Contemporary's

WORD POWER

Spelling and Vocabulary in Context

Intermediate

2

McGraw Hill · Wright Group

Acknowledgments

Page 122: Pronunciation key © 1996 by Houghton Mifflin Company. Reproduced by permission from *The American Heritage Student Dictionary*.

Series Developer
Phil LeFaivre
    Cottage Communications
    Sandwich, Massachusetts

Series Reviewer
Joan Loncich
    Instructor, Adult Basic Education
    Barnstable Community Schools
    Hyannis, Massachusetts

 **Wright Group**

ISBN: 0-8092-0837-7

Send all inquiries to:
Wright Group/McGraw-Hill
130 East Randolph Street, Suite 400
Chicago, Illinois 60601

Printed in the United States of America.

09 10 11 12 13 14 15 GB 15 14

The **McGraw·Hill** Companies

Market Development Manager

Noreen Lopez

Editorial Development Director

Cynthia Krejcsi

Project Manager

Laurie Duncan

Interior Design and Production

PiperStudiosInc

Cover Design

Kristy Sheldon

Word Power
Table of Contents

Page

To the Teacher **6**

How to Study a Word **9**

Pre-test **10**

Unit 1: Consumer Economics

Lesson 1   Money in the Bank **12**

Lesson 2   Rules for Renters **16**

Lesson 3   The Smart Shopper **20**

Lesson 4   Car Sense **24**

Unit 1 Review **28**

Unit 2: Health

Lesson 5   Doctor's Orders **30**

Lesson 6   Safety Tips **34**

Lesson 7   Exercise and Good Health **38**

Lesson 8   Keep Smiling **42**

Unit 2 Review **46**

Unit 3: Employment

Lesson 9   On the Job **48**

Lesson 10 Getting Ahead in Your Job **52**

Lesson 11 Keeping Up on the Job **56**

Lesson 12 Getting a Job **60**

Unit 3 Review **64**

Unit 4: Community Resources

Lesson 13 Days and Months 66

Lesson 14 Getting Help 70

Lesson 15 The Holiday Spirit 74

Lesson 16 Making an Emergency Call 78

Unit 4 Review 82

Unit 5: Government and Law

Lesson 17 The Roots of Democracy 84

Lesson 18 Reducing Waste 88

Lesson 19 It's the Law 92

Lesson 20 The Branches of Government 96

Unit 5 Review 100

Unit 6: Learning to Learn

Lesson 21 Plan for Success 102

Lesson 22 Learning from Mistakes 106

Lesson 23 Using Time Well 110

Lesson 24 New Ideas 114

Unit 6 Review 118

Post-test 120

How to Use the Dictionary 122

Mini-Dictionary 123

Personal Word List 133

Alphabetical Word List 134

Answer Key 137

Scoring Chart 144

To the Teacher

Goals of the Series

Word Power provides the mature learner with a systematic program of instruction for reading, writing, and spelling the words needed on the job, at home, and in the community. The vocabulary is arranged thematically at appropriate levels of difficulty and presented in meaningful contexts.

Key Features

1. Word Power *provides instruction at five levels of difficulty, so you can select the book that precisely fits your students' needs.*

Each of the five *Word Power* books is keyed to a level of the *Tests of Adult Basic Education*, Forms 7 and 8. *Word Power Introductory* correlates with Level L. *Word Power Intermediate 1* and *Intermediate 2* are tied to TABE levels E and M. *Advanced 1* and *Advanced 2* match levels D and A. The four upper-level books offer a pre-test to confirm appropriateness of level and to provide a comparison for post-test purposes.

2. *Words are presented in meaningful contexts. Students immediately see the importance of what they are studying and become motivated to complete the work successfully.*

Units in the four upper level books are keyed to one of six Comprehensive Adult Student Assessment System (CASAS) Life Skills Competencies: Consumer Economics, Health, Employment, Community Resources, Government and Law, and Learning to Learn.

3. *The skills of reading, writing, and spelling are synchronized to facilitate learning and build a portfolio of successful work.*

Once students have analyzed the meaning and spelling of the words, they can apply what they have learned in a practical writing and proofreading exercise. A number of the letters, announcements, or similar realistic messages that students write can be mailed or kept in a portfolio of each student's work.

4. *Regular review tests in standardized testing formats allow you to monitor progress while familiarizing your students with the testing strategies they will find in typical GED exams and tests of adult basic skills.*

Every four-lesson unit concludes with a two-page review test. It checks each student's progress in mastering the meaning and spelling of the words. The testing formats match those used by the TABE.

5. *The easy-to-use format and a Mini-Dictionary at the four upper levels empower students to take control of their learning and work with a high degree of independence.*

Each lesson follows a sequence through four key stages of learning, which are described on page 8. Students can work independently and progress at their own rate.

6. *The important* Introductory *book provides basic instruction in the key phonetic principles and mechanics skills in a meaningful, adult context.*

Unlike most programs for mature learners, *Word Power* provides instruction in the basic principles of sounds and letters, and it accomplishes this through high-interest, mature content.

Using the Intermediate 2 Book

Like all the books in this series, *Intermediate 2* consists of twenty-four lessons. After each unit of four lessons, a review test is provided to check progress. Each lesson is divided into four one-page parts. Each part brings to closure a coherent step in the learning process. Depending on your students and your instructional time block, one or more parts or an entire lesson might constitute a class session.

The reading level in this book has been carefully controlled, but students may need occasional help with the text. One practical strategy is to work with groups of students, reading the directions aloud to them as they follow along.

The Pre-test on pages 10 and 11 will provide assistance in evaluating how much your students know and placing them in the appropriate *Word Power* text. No single test, however, should serve as the sole guide to placement. Used in conjunction with other tests of reading and writing, as well as your own observations, this Pre-test can serve as a valuable resource. These tests have a multiple-choice format. Random guessing will result in a number of correct answers, so it is wise to expect a high level of mastery before deciding to move students to the next level. In addition, the lessons in this text include many related language skills not covered in the Pre-tests. A better strategy might be to allow students who do well on the Pre-test to progress through the lessons independently at an accelerated pace.

The Post-test on pages 120 and 121 can serve as a handy tool for checking progress. Both tests cover selected words in this text, so a comparison of scores will provide a gauge of each student's progress.

In addition to the Pre-test and Post-test, each text includes a Personal Word List page and a How to Use the Dictionary page. The Personal Word List page allows students to record words encountered outside the classroom. These words can be studied using the steps in How to Study a Word on page 9. They can also be shared and discussed with the class as a means of enhancing each lesson. This is usually best done as part of the writing and proofreading part of the lesson.

The instructions for completing each part are clearly stated and could be performed by many students with a high degree of independence. You may prefer to have students check their own work using the Answer Key on pages 137 through 143. They can record the number correct in the space provided at the bottom of most pages.

As you can see, *Word Power* is an effective and practical tool for addressing the needs of a wide variety of adult learners. We feel confident that *Word Power* will make a significant contribution to your vital work as a teacher.

Breaking Down a Lesson

Each lesson in *Word Power* progresses through the following stages of instruction:

Ⓐ Check the Meaning

Here students read the words in the context of a brief essay related to the unit theme. Students are asked to infer the meanings of the words from the context and match them with one of the definitions provided in the exercise items. These exercises, like most of the exercises in the lessons, lend themselves easily to both independent and cooperative learning.

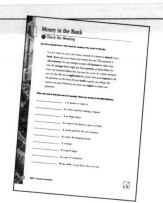

Ⓑ Study the Spelling

This page contains a wide variety of exercises designed to focus attention on the letters and word parts that make up the spelling of each word. Emphasis is placed on noting coherent clusters of letters, tricky sound/letter combinations, and related and inflected forms of the words.

Ⓒ Build Your Skills

Using one or more of the list words as a springboard, this part focuses attention on important language skills, such as recognizing homophones, inflectional endings, prefixes, suffixes, capitalization, and punctuation. Practice activities follow a concise statement of the rule and examples.

Ⓓ Proofread and Write

The lessons conclude by having students apply what they have learned. First students proofread an example of writing related to the lesson theme. Then they correct the errors they find. This is followed by a structured writing assignment modeled on the format they have just proofread. They proofread and correct their own work and make a final copy for their writing portfolios. Cooperative learning strategies can be employed by having students share a draft of their written work with a classmate and solicit his or her response before making the final copy.

How to Study a Word

Follow these steps for learning how to spell new words.

1 **Look**
at the word.

- How many syllables does it have?
- Do you know what the word means?

2 **Say**
the word aloud.

- What vowel sounds do you hear?
- What consonant sounds do you hear?

3 **Cover**
the word.

- Can you see the word in your mind?
- What are the sounds and letters in the word?

4 **Write**
the word.

- How is each sound spelled?
- Can you form the letters carefully?

5 **Check**
the spelling.

- Did you spell the word correctly?

6 If you make a mistake,
repeat the steps.

Pre-test

Part 1: Meaning

For each item below, fill in the letter next to the word or phrase that most nearly expresses the meaning of the first word.

Sample

1. hammer
- Ⓐ part of the arm
- ⬤ a tool used for driving nails
- Ⓑ a type of vegetable
- Ⓓ to mix thoroughly

---

1. credit
- Ⓐ any important paper
- Ⓒ a foolish suggestion
- Ⓑ trust that a buyer can pay for something
- Ⓓ a lengthy explanation of one's beliefs

2. absorb
- Ⓐ to hold back; to refuse
- Ⓒ a large, empty space
- Ⓑ to put an end to; finish
- Ⓓ to soak up

3. random
- Ⓐ to push with great force
- Ⓒ without a plan
- Ⓑ the harmful rays of the sun
- Ⓓ dizzy

4. modem
- Ⓐ a device often used with computers
- Ⓒ a type of sea shell
- Ⓑ a style of art
- Ⓓ modern

5. enact
- Ⓐ to cast a spell
- Ⓒ to react
- Ⓑ to make into law
- Ⓓ to pretend

6. habitat
- Ⓐ an action done over and over
- Ⓒ a program to teach skills
- Ⓑ the clothing worn by certain religious groups
- Ⓓ where an animal lives or grows

7. advocate
- Ⓐ to promote
- Ⓒ to request a favor
- Ⓑ a dishonest person
- Ⓓ a tool used to measure distances

8. strenuous
- Ⓐ stringy
- Ⓒ unusually long and narrow
- Ⓑ requiring great strength
- Ⓓ not known; unfamiliar

9. consequence
- Ⓐ happening as the result of something else
- Ⓒ the winner of a battle
- Ⓑ a prize
- Ⓓ the members of a church

10. merchandise
- Ⓐ a type of cloth
- Ⓒ an ocean vessel
- Ⓑ a dangerous journey
- Ⓓ things bought and sold

GO ON ➡

Part 2: Spelling

For each item below, fill in the letter next to the correct spelling of the word.

11. (A) success   (C) sucess
    (B) suces   (D) suscess

12. (A) complane   (C) complain
    (B) conplain   (D) complan

13. (A) chalenge   (C) challange
    (B) challunge   (D) challenge

14. (A) committe   (C) committee
    (B) comittee   (D) comite

15. (A) defents   (C) difense
    (B) defens   (D) defense

16. (A) constitution (C) constatution
    (B) constitusion   (D) constetution

17. (A) Wensday   (C) Wednesday
    (B) Wedsenday   (D) Wenesdey

18. (A) dedacate   (C) dedecate
    (B) dedicate   (D) didicate

19. (A) interview   (C) intervue
    (B) intraview   (D) innerview

20. (A) intrest   (C) interast
    (B) interist   (D) interest

21. (A) decieve   (C) deceive
    (B) daceive   (D) diceive

22. (A) applicasion (C) applacation
    (B) application   (D) aplication

23. (A) conscent   (C) consent
    (B) consint   (D) comsent

24. (A) residant   (C) residint
    (B) risident   (D) resident

25. (A) occasional (C) occasionel
    (B) occassional   (D) ocasional

26. (A) prascription (C) prescrition
    (B) prescribion   (D) prescription

27. (A) athalete   (C) athlete
    (B) athlet   (D) athelete

28. (A) Febuary   (C) February
    (B) Febuery   (D) Februery

29. (A) emergancy   (C) emergencey
    (B) emergency   (D) emergincy

30. (A) government (C) goverment
    (B) govermant   (D) geverment

Money in the Bank

Ⓐ Check the Meaning

Read the paragraph below. Think about the meaning of the words in bold type.

It is not smart to carry your money around. It is better to **deposit** it in a **bank.** Banks pay you to keep your money for you. This payment is called **interest.** So your savings account will **increase** in value every year. An **average** bank might pay three **percent,** or three dollars for every one hundred dollars that you save for a year. As a bank customer, you can also fill out an **application** for a loan. You must **respond** to all the questions on the form. If your **credit** is good, you will get the money you need. However, you must not **neglect** to make your payments.

Write each word in bold type next to its meaning. Check your answers in the Mini-Dictionary.

_____ **1.** to answer or reply to

_____ **2.** a form used for making a request

_____ **3.** to forget about

_____ **4.** to put or lay down; to put in a bank

_____ **5.** money paid for the use of money

_____ **6.** a place for keeping money

_____ **7.** ordinary

_____ **8.** to grow larger

_____ **9.** a part of a hundred

_____ **10.** the ability to pay back what you owe

B Study the Spelling

Word List

respond	increase	neglect	average	credit
percent	interest	application	bank	deposit

Add the missing letters. Write the words.

1. a___er___ge _____

4. n___g ___ ___ct _____

2. in___r___a___e _____

5. ___e___o___it _____

3. cr___d___t _____

6. r___sp___ ___d _____

Write the list word or words that fit each clue.

7. It has four syllables. _____

8. It has one syllable. _____

9. These two words begin with *in*.

_____   _____

10. You can find the word *cent* in this word. _____

Form a list word by adding letters from the first column to letters from the second column. Write the list word. The first one is done for you.

de	it
ne	spond
cred	posit
per	glect
re	cent

11. _deposit_____

12. _____

13. _____

14. _____

15. _____

Ⓒ Build Your Skills

 Language Tutor

Add -s to most words to make them plural.

one bank . . . . several ban<u>ks</u>   his dime . . . . . a handful of dime<u>s</u>

my application . . . many application<u>s</u>   a customer . . . . a lot of customer<u>s</u>

Add -es to words ending with s, x, ch, or sh.

one glass . . . . several glass<u>es</u>   one mailbox . . two mailbox<u>es</u>

our beach . . . . . . many beach<u>es</u>   a wish . . . . two wish<u>es</u>

Add -s or -es to these words to make them plural.

1. dollar _____

2. window _____

3. bus _____

4. form _____

5. church _____

6. page _____

7. hour _____

8. dish _____

9. fox _____

10. average _____

Read each sentence. Choose the word from the box that best completes each sentence.

Write the correct form of the word–singular or plural–in the blank.

box	loan	check	tax	question

11. Last month I wrote ten _____ to pay my bills.

12. My bank will make us a _____ to buy a car.

13. The application listed ten _____ for us to answer.

14. You must pay a sales _____ when buying a car.

15. Many people rent _____ in the bank's safe.

D Proofread and Write

Here is a list of things Hank wanted to ask someone at the bank. He made four spelling mistakes. He also made a mistake in singular and plural form. Cross out the misspelled words. Write the correct spellings above them.

Things to Ask the Bank

Will your bank pay interests on my savings every month?

What parcent are you now paying on savings?

Do you think interest rates will increase soon?

Is there a way to deposit money when the bank is closed?

Where can I get an applacation for a loan?

How long does it take you to rispond to a loan request?

Can I get a credit card through your bank?

What is the avrage time you give to pay back a loan?

Make a list of questions to ask someone at your bank. Use at least four list words.

_____

_____

_____

_____

_____

_____

Writing Portfolio

Proofread your questions carefully and correct any mistakes. Then make a clean copy and put it in your writing portfolio.

Rules for Renters

A Check the Meaning

Read the paragraph below. Think about the meaning of the words in bold type.

It is wise to know the rules when you rent an **apartment**. A good renter, or **resident**, takes care of the owner's **property**. Always clean the stove and other things in the **kitchen** as soon as they get dirty. Get the owner's **consent** before painting anything. Some owners will even give you the paint. If something is broken, tell the manager. He or she should **offer** to fix it right away. It is easier to fix a problem when it is small. Do not wait until it becomes **enormous**. Also, park your car only where your **permit** says you can. Do not park in any empty space just because it is **vacant**. If you do, your neighbors will **complain**, and you may have to pay a fine.

Write each word in bold type next to its meaning. Check your answers in the Mini-Dictionary.

_____ **1.** a license or similar paper that shows you have permission to do something

_____ **2.** a room where food is cooked

_____ **3.** to point out a problem or something that is wrong

_____ **4.** a room or group of rooms to live in, usually a part of a large building

_____ **5.** to show that you are willing to do something

_____ **6.** very large

_____ **7.** something one owns

_____ **8.** a person who lives in a given place

_____ **9.** empty

_____ **10.** permission

B Study the Spelling

Word List

vacant	apartment	resident	offer	permit
kitchen	complain	property	enormous	consent

Write the words with three syllables. Draw a line between the syllables.

1. _____ 3. _____

2. _____ 4. _____

Form a list word by adding letters from the first column to letters from the second column. Write the list word.

com	cant	5. _____
con	ident	6. _____
per	sent	7. _____
va	mit	8. _____
res	plain	9. _____

Write the list word for each clue.

10. It has a double consonant in its spelling. _____

11. It has the word *kit* in its spelling. _____

12. It begins with the short i sound you hear in *it*. _____

13. It ends with the long e sound spelled with a *y*. _____

14. It ends with *ant*. _____

15. It comes from the word *reside*, meaning to live in a place. _____

16. It has the word *plain* in its spelling. _____

17. It ends with *ous*. _____

One word in each group is misspelled. Circle the misspelled word. Write it correctly.

18. complane   enormous   vacant   _____

19. consent   permit   residant   _____

20. kitchen   appartment   property   _____

C Build Your Skills

Language Tutor

Some words have "extra" letters, called silent letters. You may not hear these letters when you say the words, but they are needed in the spelling.

kitchen   knee   half   wrong   listen   comb   could

Say each word; then write it on the line. Circle any silent letters.

1. knight _____

2. wrap _____

3. calf _____

4. bomb _____

5. latch _____

6. should _____

7. itch _____

8. fasten _____

9. knit _____

10. wrist _____

11. limb _____

12. talk _____

Copy the sentences. Add the missing letters.

13. Use an iron to smooth out the ___rinkle in the shirt.

_____

14. We asked the landlord to put a new la___ch on our door.

_____

15. The storm broke a lim___ from the tree.

_____

16. An atomic bom___ was dropped on Japan on August 6, 1945.

_____

17. The insect bite made my skin i___ch all day.

_____

18. We must ta___k to him about the lack of parking.

_____

Score: _____ / 18

D Proofread and Write

Matt got the following list of rules with his lease. The list has four spelling mistakes. Cross out the misspelled words. Write the correct spelling above them.

Woodside Apartments

Rules for Renters

- Only cars with a permit on the rear window may be parked in the lot.

- You must be a residant of these apartments to use the pool.

- We will offer you the chance to move to any apartment that becomes vacent.

- The smoke alarm in the kitchen must be kept on at all times.

- Renters will be charged for damage to apartment propurty.

- No pets are allowed without the conscent of the manager.

- All renters have the right to complain to the manager. This should always be done in writing.

José Lopez

Manager

Writing Portfolio

Suppose you lived in the Woodside Apartments. Write a letter to Mr. Lopez about one or more of the rules. You can ask for more information or tell him about a problem you are having. Use at least four list words.

Proofread your letter carefully and correct any mistakes. Then make a clean copy and put it in your writing portfolio.

The Smart Shopper

Ⓐ Check the Meaning

Read the paragraph below. Think about the meaning of the words in bold type.

Whether on a **billboard** or in a newspaper, ads can **deceive** even the best shoppers. The only protection against trickery is a thorough **knowledge** of the **merchandise** and a desire to save money. Always **compare** prices. For example, having a **coupon** worth $1.00 on one brand is no bargain if another brand costs $2.00 less.

BIG SALE: MEN'S SHOES JUST $30.00

Would you buy these or go across the street? There the **charge** for shoes is two pairs for $40.00. If you spent $30.00 for a pair, return the shoes and ask the store manager to **refund** your **money**. To be a **success** at shopping, you must watch every penny.

Write each word in bold type next to its meaning. Check your answers in the Mini-Dictionary.

_____ **1.** to examine what is alike and different about two things

_____ **2.** to give back

_____ **3.** to mislead or to cheat

_____ **4.** an understanding of facts, ideas, or information

_____ **5.** the amount asked for as payment

_____ **6.** the coins or bills used to pay for things

_____ **7.** things that are bought and sold

_____ **8.** a large board used for outdoor advertising

_____ **9.** a person who gets the results he or she wants

_____ **10.** piece of paper used to get something of value

B Study the Spelling

Word List

success	compare	coupon	refund	charge
merchandise	billboard	deceive	money	knowledge

Write the list word for each clue.

1. It has two sets of double consonants. _____

2. It is made from two shorter words. _____

3. It begins with a silent *k*. _____

4. It has three syllables. _____

5. It begins with *re–*. _____

6. It ends with a long e sound spelled *ey*. _____

7. The long e sound in the middle of this word is spelled *ei*.

_____

8. It begins like *chip* and ends like *large*. _____

Add the missing syllable. Write the list word.

9. suc_____ _____

10. de_____ _____

11. _____pon _____

12. knowl_____ _____

13. re_____ _____

14. bill_____ _____

Write the list word that would come between each pair of words in a dictionary.

15. minute _____ music

16. cute _____ drive

17. jamboree _____ labor

18. rush _____ wagon

19. angry _____ bumper

20. cent _____ churn

Score: / 20

C Build Your Skills

Language Tutor

You can make new words by simply adding *-ed* and *-ing* to most words.

refund + -ed = refunded   refund + -ing = refunding

Add *-ed* or *-ing* to these words.

1. deliver + -ed = _____

2. sing + -ing = _____

3. allow + -ed = _____

4. cough + -ed = _____

5. jump + -ing = _____

6. brush + -ed = _____

7. call + -ed = _____

8. seek + -ing = _____

9. send + -ing = _____

10. follow + -ed = _____

11. tell + -ing = _____

12. paint + -ing = _____

Write each sentence. Add *-ed* or *-ing* to the underlined word.

13. The clerk asked me to stop <u>pinch</u> the lemons.

_____

14. I will not buy a <u>spoil</u> can of beans.

_____

15. The cashier <u>redeem</u> my coupons.

_____

16. Are they <u>return</u> this item for the newer ones?

_____

17. The deadline was <u>extend</u> to the end of the week.

_____

18. I am <u>try</u> to get the most for each dollar I spend.

_____

19. You should be <u>thrill</u> with the bargains I found.

_____

20. I am still <u>think</u> about which item to buy.

_____

Ⓓ Proofread and Write

This article appeared in a magazine. The writer made three spelling mistakes and one mistake in adding *-ing*. Cross out the misspelled words and the word with the *-ing* mistake. Write the correct spellings above them.

Dare to Compare

What does a store do when it is stuck with merchandize that will not sell? It raises the price, then gives away cuepons that are supposed to save you money. This is a way of trickinng you into thinking you found a good buy. Don't fall for it. Go to several stores. Compare prices. Knowlege is everything.

Save
$1.00
off your next purchase
$1 $1 $1 $1

Write some advice for shopping. You might want to make a list of Dos and Don'ts for shopping at a supermarket. Use at least four list words.

_____

_____

_____

_____

_____

_____

_____

 Writing Portfolio

Proofread your advice carefully and correct any mistakes. Then make a clean copy and put it in your writing portfolio.

Car Sense

Ⓐ Check the Meaning

Read the paragraph below. Think about the meaning of the words in bold type.

A good car is not just a car with a low price. There are other things to consider. It should get good **mileage** on each **gallon** of fuel, so that you spend less money on **gasoline**. A car that travels thirty miles on a gallon of gas costs far less to run than a car that goes only fifteen miles on a gallon. A **practical** car will not **break** often, and a small bump will not **damage** its body. You should be able to keep a car like this in good **condition** without spending too much money. A car that is always in and out of the **garage** is not a good buy. You can find information about **foreign** and American cars in any library. Look for **special** books called buyers' guides. These have facts about cars, including how often each kind needs to be serviced.

Write each word in bold type next to its meaning. Check your answers in the Mini-Dictionary.

_____ **1.** the fuel for cars and trucks

_____ **2.** to harm or hurt

_____ **3.** the number of miles traveled

_____ **4.** a place where cars are fixed or stored

_____ **5.** state of fitness; shape

_____ **6.** intended for a certain purpose; not like others

_____ **7.** sensible; useful

_____ **8.** not from one's own country

_____ **9.** a unit of measure; four quarts of a liquid

_____ **10.** to fail or to stop working

B Study the Spelling

Word List

gasoline	damage	foreign	practical	special
break	mileage	garage	condition	gallon

Write the list word or words for each clue.

1. It contains the word *gas*. _____

2. It contains the word *mile*. _____

3. It contains the word *for*. _____

4. It contains a double *l*. _____

5. It ends with *cial*. _____

6. It rhymes with *take*. _____

7. They end with *age*.

_____ _____ _____

8. It has just one syllable. _____

Replace the underlined letters to write a list word.

9. tradition _____ **11.** steak _____

10. practiced _____ **12.** average _____

Write the list words that contain three syllables. Draw lines between the syllables.

13. _____

14. _____

15. _____

Add the missing letters. Write the list word.

16. for___ ___gn _____ **19.** spe___i___l _____

17. gas___l___ne _____ **20.** ga___ ___on _____

18. br___ ___k _____

© Build Your Skills

Language Tutor

Some words sound the same, but they do not have the same spelling or meaning.

The glass window will <u>break</u> if you hit it.
Step on the <u>brake</u> to stop the car.

Study the the meaning of the underlined words in these sentences.

I had to <u>wait</u> an hour for the bus.
His <u>weight</u> dropped by ten pounds.

I enjoy the <u>peace</u> and quiet of the library.
Joan ate the last <u>piece</u> of apple pie.

The <u>scent</u> of burnt toast filled the kitchen.
Norm <u>sent</u> a check to the power company.

I will need a <u>loan</u> to buy that stove.
A <u>lone</u> actor entered the stage.

<u>Their</u> dog barked all night.
I went <u>there</u> last week.
<u>They're</u> going to take a bus to New York.

Write the word in parentheses that fits each sentence.

1. I love the _____ of pine trees in the forest. (scent; sent)

2. I cannot _____ any longer or I will be late. (wait; weight)

3. I always buy gasoline _____ because it costs less. (their; there; they're)

4. A _____ of the tree fell on the garage. (peace; piece)

5. Jim was the _____ winner of the best worker award. (loan; lone)

6. Has anyone _____ in the coupon? (scent; sent)

7. The Wangs left _____ car in the driveway. (their; there; they're)

8. The _____ of the load flattened the tire. (wait; weight)

9. The car _____ must be paid back in twenty-four months. (loan; lone)

10. All nations must work for a lasting _____. (peace; piece)

Score: /10

Ⓓ Proofread and Write

Katrina saw two used cars for sale. She made a chart to compare them. Her chart has four spelling mistakes in it. Cross out the misspelled words. Write the correct spellings above them.

	Car on Elm Street	Car on Second Ave.
cost	$2400	$2600
kind	four-door sedan	two-door
foreign?	no	yes
conditon	dented bumper; did not damaje fender	seems perfect
specail features	kept in a garage	gets good milage

What would you look for in a car? List the things you think a good car should have.
Use at least four list words.

_____

_____

_____

_____

_____

_____

_____

 Writing Portfolio

Proofread your list carefully and correct any mistakes. Make a clean copy and put it in your writing portfolio or use your list to help you buy a car.

Unit 1 Review

Complete the Meaning

Fill in the circle next to the word that best completes each sentence.

Sample

The plane will be late. The _____ was caused by bad weather.

- (A) rain
- ● delay
- (C) worry
- (D) anger

1. Mary Lou called four banks. She wants the highest _____ rate for her savings.

   - (A) interest
   - (B) deposit
   - (C) average
   - (D) coupon

2. Not all brands are the same price. It is smart to _____ prices.

   - (A) neglect
   - (B) offer
   - (C) damage
   - (D) compare

3. She took a second job. This will _____ her income.

   - (A) refund
   - (B) vanish
   - (C) increase
   - (D) damage

4. Before buying a used item, check the _____ carefully.

   - (A) billboard
   - (B) percent
   - (C) condition
   - (D) application

5. The landlord cannot simply enter your home. He must have your _____.

   - (A) consent
   - (B) success
   - (C) money
   - (D) coupon

6. No one had seen anyone there for a long time. The house had been _____ for weeks.

   - (A) fortunate
   - (B) enormous
   - (C) vacant
   - (D) practical

7. After the accident, they took the car to the shop and repaired the _____.

   - (A) garage
   - (B) credit
   - (C) damage
   - (D) money

8. A letter to San Juan takes from four to six days to arrive. The _____ time is five days.

   - (A) vacant
   - (B) average
   - (C) enormous
   - (D) practical

9. Only those who live here may use the pool. You must be a(n) _____.

   - (A) resident
   - (B) kitchen
   - (C) apartment
   - (D) property

10. Always read the small print in a newspaper ad. Some ads try to _____ you by hiding some facts.

    - (A) neglect
    - (B) charge
    - (C) compare
    - (D) deceive

GO ON ➡

Check the Spelling

Fill in the circle next to the word that is spelled correctly and best completes each sentence.

11. I wrote Jean a letter, but she didn't _____.

Ⓐ raspond
Ⓒ respund
Ⓑ respond
Ⓓ respound

12. Ed's _____ of motors is impressive.

Ⓐ knowledge
Ⓒ knouledge
Ⓑ knowlege
Ⓓ knowladge

13. Our car gets good _____ on the highway.

Ⓐ milage
Ⓒ milege
Ⓑ mileage
Ⓓ mialege

14. We cooked a big dinner in the _____.

Ⓐ kichen
Ⓒ kitchin
Ⓑ kitchan
Ⓓ kitchen

15. We filled the tank with _____ before we left for our trip.

Ⓐ gasoline
Ⓒ gasalene
Ⓑ gasolene
Ⓓ gasolein

16. A _____ of milk costs $2.00 at that store.

Ⓐ galon
Ⓒ gallen
Ⓑ gallon
Ⓓ galun

17. On our trip we visited several _____ countries.

Ⓐ foriegn
Ⓒ fareign
Ⓑ foreign
Ⓓ forein

18. We wanted to make his birthday a _____ day for him.

Ⓐ special
Ⓒ speciel
Ⓑ speshal
Ⓓ specal

19. A renter has the right to _____ to his landlord.

Ⓐ complane
Ⓒ complein
Ⓑ cumplain
Ⓓ complain

20. My favorite store has just received some new _____.

Ⓐ merchandize
Ⓒ merchantize
Ⓑ merchandise
Ⓓ merchandice

STOP

Score: _____ / 20

5 Doctor's Orders

Ⓐ Check the Meaning

Read the paragraphs below. Think about the meaning of the words in bold type.

All of us have an **ache** from time to time. You do not need to do anything about an **occasional** pain. However, if something hurts all the time, you may need to see a **doctor** or go to a **hospital**. Do this if the pain is **extreme** or if it lasts a long time.

A doctor can write a **prescription**, an order for one kind of medicine. The medicine could be something you drink or a **tablet** you take. The doctor will tell you the **exact** amount to take and when to take it. Medicines can be **dangerous**, so be sure you follow the doctor's orders. You do not want the medicine to **poison** you. Ask questions if you need help.

Write each word in bold type next to its meaning. Check your answers in the Mini-Dictionary.

_____ **1.** a place where sick or injured people are treated

_____ **2.** happening from time to time

_____ **3.** very bad or very great

_____ **4.** a pill

_____ **5.** able to harm

_____ **6.** pain

_____ **7.** no more or less than a certain amount

_____ **8.** to harm or destroy through chemical action

_____ **9.** a written order for a medicine

_____ **10.** someone trained to identify and treat illness or injuries

B Study the Spelling

Word List

ache	doctor	occasional	extreme	tablet
dangerous	exact	hospital	prescription	poison

Write a list word or words for each clue.

1. It has one syllable. _____

2. It has four syllables. _____

3. These two words begin with *ex*.

_____   _____

4. It comes from the word *prescribe*. _____

5. It contains the word *tab*. _____

6. It contains the word *danger*. _____

7. It has three syllables and ends with *al*. _____

Add the missing letters. Write the list word.

8. p___is___n _____   12. ac___ ___ _____

9. d___ct___r _____   13. extr___m___ _____

10. e___ ___ct _____   14. hosp___t___l _____

11. tab___ ___t _____   15. o___ca___ion___l _____

One word in each group is misspelled. Circle the misspelled word. Write it correctly.

16. ocasional   dangerous   doctor   _____

17. tablet   pioson   exact   _____

18. extreme   doctor   perscription   _____

19. acke   exact   extreme   _____

20. dangerous   tablet   hospitel   _____

C Build Your Skills

Language Tutor

Add **-ed** and **-ing** to most words to make new words.

When a word ends with **e**, the **e** is usually dropped before adding **-ed** or **-ing**.

jump + -ed = jumped   jump + -ing = jumping
ache + -ed = ached   ache + -ing = aching

Add the endings to the words. Write the new words.

1. brush + -ing = _____   **7.** play + -ing = _____

2. date + -ed = _____   **8.** move + -ed = _____

3. charge + -ed = _____   **9.** share + -ed = _____

4. lift + -ed = _____   **10.** lose + -ing = _____

5. write + -ing = _____   **11.** open + -ed = _____

6. drive + -ing = _____   **12.** use + -ing = _____

Copy each sentence. Add -ed or -ing to the underlined word.

13. I <u>save</u> the bottle that the pills came in.

_____

14. You should not be <u>share</u> your pills with anyone else.

_____

15. We will be <u>give</u> John three pills a day.

_____

16. Keep this cough syrup <u>store</u> in a cool place.

_____

17. I <u>place</u> the pills where the baby could not get them.

_____

18. Have you <u>taste</u> this yet?

_____

Score: /18

D Proofread and Write

Janet wrote this note to her son's teacher. She made four spelling mistakes, including a mistake in adding *-ed* or *-ing*. Cross out the misspelled words. Write the correct spellings above them.

September 14, 1997

Dear Mr. Farmer:

My son, Jim, was home last week. He had a tooth pulled and his mouth still had a bad acke. Our doctur said he did not need a prescription. An ocasional pain pill from the drugstore was all he needed. Please remind Jim to take one pill with lunch. He will be takeing the rest at home.

Thanks for your help.

Sincerely,

Janet Kim

Janet Kim

Writing Portfolio

Write a note to a teacher. Use your own paper. Ask the teacher to excuse you or your child because of an illness. Use at least four list words.

Proofread your note carefully and correct any mistakes. Then make a clean copy and put it in your writing portfolio.

6 Safety Tips

Ⓐ Check the Meaning

Read the paragraph below. Think about the meaning of the words in bold type.

No one plans to have an **accident**, but accidents still happen. They happen when people are careless. They also happen when people are **sleepy** or too tired to be **aware** of certain dangers. These tips can help keep your home safer:

1. Use paper towels to pick up **broken** glass. Paper towels **absorb** the liquid and keep your hands safe from cuts.

2. Don't ever put medicine into a food **bottle**. Someone might mistake **iodine** for food. People can die or become sick if they **swallow** a medicine.

3. Keep the food you eat safe from germs. Cook food thoroughly. **Chill** leftovers in a cold refrigerator.

4. Keep a first-aid kit in your home. Let only **trustworthy** people use it.

Write each word in bold type next to its meaning. Check your answers in the Mini-Dictionary.

_____ **1.** to keep cold

_____ **2.** to pass something from the mouth to the stomach

_____ **3.** knowing or understanding

_____ **4.** tired or drowsy

_____ **5.** something that was not planned

_____ **6.** a container for liquids

_____ **7.** to soak up

_____ **8.** damaged or not working well

_____ **9.** a kind of medicine

_____ **10.** dependable; able to be trusted

Score: /10

B Study the Spelling

Word List

accident	swallow	bottle	sleepy	chill
absorb	trustworthy	aware	broken	iodine

Write the list words that contain double consonants. Draw a line between the double consonants.

1. _____ 3. _____

2. _____ 4. _____

Each word below is made from a list word. Write the list word.

5. bottled _____ 8. accidentally _____

6. unbroken _____ 9. chillier _____

7. sleepiness _____ 10. trustworthiness _____

Write the list word for each clue.

11. It comes from the word *sleep*. _____

12. It contains the words *trust* and *worthy*. _____

13. It comes from the word *broke*. _____

14. It rhymes with *fill*. _____

15. The word *absorbent* comes from this word. _____

16. The word *accidental* comes from this word. _____

17. It rhymes with *creepy*. _____

18. It has just one syllable. _____

19. It has several letters and four vowels. _____

Write the list words with three syllables. Draw lines between the syllables.

20. _____ 22. _____

21. _____

© Build Your Skills

Language Tutor

A prefix is a word part put at the beginning of a word. It changes the meaning of the word.
The prefix *un-* adds the meaning "not" or "opposite."
The prefix *re-* adds the meaning "back" or "again."

un- + broken = unbroken, meaning "not broken"
re- + broken = rebroken, meaning "broken again"

Add the prefix that means "not" or "opposite" to these words. Write the words.

1. ___ ___fair _____

2. ___ ___happy _____

3. ___ ___common _____

4. ___ ___believable _____

5. ___ ___able _____

6. ___ ___cover _____

7. ___ ___like _____

8. ___ ___wanted _____

9. ___ ___equal _____

10. ___ ___kind _____

11. ___ ___known _____

12. ___ ___usual _____

Use the prefix that means "back" or "again" to write a word for each meaning below.

13. to wrap again _____

14. to cycle again _____

15. to view again _____

16. to call again _____

17. to join again _____

18. to enter again _____

Add the word with *re-* or *un-* from the exercises above that fits each sentence. Then write another sentence using that word again.

19. I will study the lesson again. I always _____ a lesson before a test.

_____

_____

20. He drives a purple car unlike any other car I've seen. It is a very
_____ sight.

_____

_____

Score: /20

Ⓓ Proofread and Write

Max works at a daycare center. He wrote this report after a child fell. He made four spelling mistakes.
Cross out the misspelled words. Write the correct spellings above them.

INJURY REPORT

Date: Monday, April 3, 1998   **Child(ren) Involved:** Tamara Gomez

Nature of Mishap: Tamara had an acident on the gym set. It happened

shortly after nap time, so she may have been a little slepy. She fell off and

banged her arm. Her arm had a small scratch on it, but it was not broaken.

Her heavy sweater absorbed some of the shock.

Action Taken: I put iodine on the cut. I wrote a note to her parents, so that

they will be awaer of what happened.

Report Filed By: Max Jensen

Writing Portfolio

Write an accident report on another piece of paper. The accident can be about anything
that happened to someone who works or studies with you. Use at least four list words.

Proofread your report carefully and correct any mistakes. Then make a clean copy and
put it in your writing portfolio.

Exercise and Good Health

Ⓐ Check the Meaning

Read the paragraphs below. Think about the meaning of the words in bold type.

Jake had been a good **athlete** when he was young. He played baseball, basketball, and **similar** team sports. He liked these **strenuous** activities because they made him feel fit and **healthy**. The doctor said it was good for his **heart**. But as Jake got older, he stopped playing sports. He began **smoking** and got short of **breath**. He began to develop a **cough**.

Then Jake took a new job. It was an **opportunity** to earn more money. This new shop wanted a clean **environment** for its workers. Smoking was not allowed, so Jake quit. His cough stopped, and he is no longer short of breath. Best of all, he lowered his chance of having heart trouble.

Write each word in bold type next to its meaning. Check your answers in the Mini-Dictionary.

_____ **1.** the body part that pumps blood

_____ **2.** the air going in and out of your lungs

_____ **3.** alike, but not exactly the same

_____ **4.** fit and strong; not ill

_____ **5.** a person who is good at sports

_____ **6.** a chance

_____ **7.** the conditions or area all around you

_____ **8.** an illness in which air or fluid is forced from the lungs

_____ **9.** taking great effort

_____ **10.** the act of taking in tobacco fumes

B Study the Spelling

Word List

athlete	strenuous	similar	breath	smoking
cough	environment	healthy	opportunity	heart

Add the missing letters. Then write the list word.

1. h___al___hy _____

2. s___mil___r _____

3. sm___k___ng _____

4. ath___ ___te _____

5. str___n___ous _____

Find the list word in each of these words. Write the list word.

6. heartless _____

7. similarity _____

8. unhealthy _____

9. breathe _____

Write the list word or words for each clue.

10. It ends with *ment*. _____

11. It has five syllables and a double consonant. _____

12. It begins like *strength* and ends with *ous*. _____

13. It ends with a long e sound spelled with a *y*. _____

14. It rhymes with *off*, but ends with *gh*. _____

15. They begin with *hea*. _____ _____

Write the three list words that begin with *s* in alphabetical order.

16. _____

17. _____

18. _____

C Build Your Skills

Language Tutor

When a word ends with a consonant and a *y*, change the *y* to *i* before adding *-es* or *-ed*.

opportunity + -es = opportunities
try + -ed = tried

Add the endings to the words.

1. worry + -es = _____

2. marry + -ed = _____

3. copy + -es = _____

4. study + -ed = _____

5. penny + -es = _____

6. cry + -ed = _____

7. baby + -es = _____

8. carry + -ed = _____

9. family + -es = _____

10. hurry + -ed = _____

11. reply + -es = _____

12. apply + -es = _____

13. empty + -ed = _____

14. puppy + -es = _____

Copy each sentence. Add *-es* or *-ed* to the underlined word.

15. Last night the athlete <u>carry</u> the torch into the arena.

_____

16. Marta washed and <u>dry</u> her hair.

_____

17. Too much <u>fry</u> food is not good for your heart.

_____

18. Sid always <u>worry</u> about his test scores, but he makes high scores.

_____

19. Several <u>family</u> offered to help us move.

_____

20. Make two <u>copy</u> of your paper so that you have an extra one.

_____

Ⓓ Proofread and Write

Kim was due for a checkup. She made a list of questions to ask her doctor. Kim made four spelling mistakes. Cross out the misspelled words. Write the correct spellings above them.

<u>Questions for Dr. Suarez</u>

Is running too strenous for a person my age? I seem to be out

of breath when I run.

Would walking be as good for my hart as running?

What are some helthy snack foods?

How much sleep do I really need?

What should I do about this cough?

Can you give me something to help me stop smokeing?

What should I do for a sore back?

Make a list of health questions that you would like to ask a doctor. Use at least four list words.

_____

_____

_____

_____

_____

_____

Writing Portfolio

Proofread your questions carefully and correct any mistakes. Then make a clean copy. Take your list on your next visit to a doctor, or put it in your writing portfolio.

Keep Smiling

Ⓐ Check the Meaning

Read the paragraph below. Think about the meaning of the words in bold type.

To keep a great smile, see a **dentist** every year. Some people even **recommend** that you go twice a year. A dentist can help you avoid the problems that **cause** tooth loss. Small bits of food can get caught between your **teeth**. This can **irritate** a tooth and cause it to **decay** and rot. Make an **appointment** before you have a problem. You need to fix the problem, or you may not like the **consequence**: lost teeth. Losing teeth can make you look and feel **miserable**. If you have not seen a dentist in the last year, you should **consult** one soon.

Write each word in bold type next to its meaning. Check your answers in the Mini-Dictionary.

_____ **1.** more than one tooth

_____ **2.** to make happen

_____ **3.** to suggest or advise

_____ **4.** an expert on the care and treatment of teeth and gums

_____ **5.** an agreement to meet at a certain time

_____ **6.** result

_____ **7.** to rot

_____ **8.** to annoy or bother

_____ **9.** to ask for suggestions or information

_____ **10.** very unhappy

B Study the Spelling

Word List

recommend	appointment	cause	consequence	decay
teeth	miserable	irritate	dentist	consult

Write the list word or words for each clue.

1. The noun *consultant* is formed from this verb. _____

2. It comes from the word *misery*. _____

3. It ends with the suffix *-ment*. _____

4. It has a double vowel. _____

5. They have double consonants.

_____ _____ _____

6. It is in the word *dentistry*. _____

7. It has the prefix *re-*. _____

8. It ends with the suffix *-able*. _____

9. They begin with *con*. _____ _____

10. It ends with a long a sound spelled *ay*. _____

Form a list word by adding letters from the first column to letters from the second and third columns. Write the list word.

11. rec	point	tate	_____
12. ir	om	quence	_____
13. con	ri	ment	_____
14. ap	se	mend	_____

One word in each group is misspelled. Circle the misspelled word and write it correctly.

15. consequence	reccommend	miserable	_____
16. teath	consult	decay	_____
17. dentist	irritate	apointment	_____
18. cauze	consult	consequence	_____

© Build Your Skills

Language Tutor

You add *-s* or *-es* to most words to make them plural. Some words form their plurals in unusual ways.

one tooth   many teeth

For each item, write the missing plural. It will be one of the words below.

men	**women**	**children**	**feet**	**loaves**
fish	**sheep**	**mice**	**geese**	**deer**

1. one mouse, many _____

2. one child, several _____

3. one loaf, three _____

4. one deer, a herd of _____

5. one man, a group of _____

6. one fish, a school of _____

7. one woman, many_____

8. one foot, a pair of _____

9. one goose, four _____

10. one sheep, several _____

Complete the puzzle by writing the plural form of each clue word. Write the word in the puzzle.

11. man

12. loaf

13. woman

14. mouse

15. child

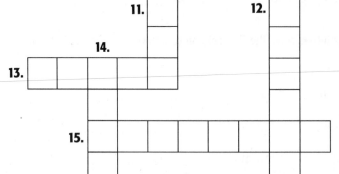

Ⓓ Proofread and Write

Lon needed time off from his job, so he wrote this memo to his crew leader. He made four spelling mistakes. Cross out the misspelled words. Write the correct spellings above them. Write in the missing capital and period.

MEMO

To: Sid Gold   **Subject:** Time off
From: Lon Dexter   **Date:** March 9, 1998

I need to ask for two hours off tomorrow morning for an appontment with my dentist. I usually connsult him on weekends. however, I need to see him quickly this time My teeth hurt, and I feel misrable. I hope Dr. Wing can find the cause of the pain. I will use my sick time. If you can allow me this time off, you will need to replace me. I recomend you ask Ramon to fill in. He knows the job well and should be free.

Writing Portfolio

On another piece of paper, write a memo asking for time off. Tell how much time you need and why you need it. Use at least four list words.

Proofread your memo and correct any misspelled words. Then make a clean copy and put it in your writing portfolio.

Unit 2 Review

Finish the Meaning

Fill in the circle next to the word that best completes each sentence.

1. Tom hurt his hand at work. We took him to the _____ to get help.

   Ⓐ kitchen　　Ⓒ bank
   Ⓑ hospital　　Ⓓ apartment

2. Laurie's boss gave her a key to the safe. Laurie must be a very _____ employee.

   Ⓐ healthy　　Ⓒ trustworthy
   Ⓑ similar　　Ⓓ average

3. I need to find a new babysitter. Do you know someone you could _____ ?

   Ⓐ recommend　　Ⓒ deposit
   Ⓑ offer　　Ⓓ complain

4. Everyone in Tina's family plays sports. Naturally, she is quite a good _____ , too.

   Ⓐ athlete　　Ⓒ resident
   Ⓑ dentist　　Ⓓ doctor

5. To make the shelf fit, Stan had to take _____ measurements.

   Ⓐ exact　　Ⓒ extreme
   Ⓑ enormous　　Ⓓ vacant

6. Call your dentist early. Sometimes it takes weeks to get an _____.

   Ⓐ prescription　　Ⓒ appointment
   Ⓑ application　　Ⓓ permit

7. That looks like a pretty bad cut on your leg. I'll get you some _____ to put on it.

   Ⓐ poison　　Ⓒ iodine
   Ⓑ decay　　Ⓓ interest

8. Kathy had such a sore throat that she could barely _____ her food.

   Ⓐ swallow　　Ⓒ deposit
   Ⓑ irritate　　Ⓓ absorb

9. The baby has been crying all day. She must be getting her first _____.

   Ⓐ opportunity　　Ⓒ property
   Ⓑ bottle　　Ⓓ teeth

10. The meat is not cold, and we have no ice cubes. I think the freezer must be _____.

    Ⓐ dangerous　　Ⓒ strenuous
    Ⓑ enormous　　Ⓓ broken

11. Wash the cleaning fluid off your hands. It will _____ your skin.

    Ⓐ irritate　　Ⓒ recommend
    Ⓑ offer　　Ⓓ absorb

12. We sat on the bus for hours. Jim had a terrible _____ in his back.

    Ⓐ chill　　Ⓒ ache
    Ⓑ cough　　Ⓓ prescription

GO ON ▶

Check the Spelling

Fill in the circle next to the word that is spelled correctly and best completes each sentence.

13. Exercise will do wonders for your
_____.

(A) haert   (C) hart
(B) heart   (D) harte

14. The police found the _____ of the fire.

(A) coz   (C) cause
(B) kause   (D) couse

15. Everyone enjoys an _____ day off.

(A) occasional   (C) occaisional
(B) ocasional   (D) occaisionel

16. The slippery road created an _____.

(A) accadent   (C) acsident
(B) axcident   (D) accident

17. Chris stopped to catch his _____ after
running up the stairs.

(A) breth   (C) breath
(B) braeth   (D) breathe

18. Before starting an exercise program,
_____ your doctor.

(A) cunsult   (C) konsult
(B) consult   (D) kunsult

19. Troy put out his cigarette when he saw
the "No _____" sign.

(A) Smocking   (C) Smokeing
(B) Smokin   (D) Smoking

20. The new packages will reduce waste
and help protect the _____.

(A) environment   (C) envirement
(B) enviroment   (D) invironment

21. After the long drive, Randy felt very
_____.

(A) slepy   (C) sleepie
(B) sleepy   (D) sleapy

22. Take an aspirin _____ for your
headache.

(A) tablet   (C) tablot
(B) tablette   (D) tahblet

23. As night fell, we became _____ of
the stars.

(A) awear   (C) awair
(B) aware   (D) awere

24. After drinking the sour milk, Ed
felt _____

(A) mizerable   (C) miserabel
(B) miserible   (D) miserable

STOP

Score: /24

On the Job

A Check the Meaning

Read the paragraph below. Think about the meaning of the words in bold type.

Before starting a job, find out your hourly pay. If you are paid a fixed amount, called a **salary**, figure out how much that comes to per hour and on an **annual** or yearly basis. Next, read any union **contract** you may receive. This agreement or other written information should state your **benefits**, such as a **retirement** plan. When you are older and unable to work for the **company**, you will need these payments. Find out about **vacation** time and other time off. Be sure to fill out a **tax** form. The answers you give on this form affect the amount of take-home pay your earnings will **yield**. Of course, you must **comply** with the law when answering tax questions.

Write each word in bold type next to its meaning. Check your answers in the Mini-Dictionary.

_____ **1.** a written agreement

_____ **2.** having to do with no longer working, often due to age

_____ **3.** time away from work for pleasure or rest

_____ **4.** to follow a request or rule

_____ **5.** to produce as a result

_____ **6.** involving money paid to the government

_____ **7.** payments for work in a form other than money

_____ **8.** yearly

_____ **9.** a business organization

_____ **10.** a fixed amount of money paid on a regular basis

Score: _____ 10

B Study the Spelling

Word List

salary	company	contract	retirement	annual
benefit	yield	comply	tax	vacation

Write a list word or words for each clue.

1. They have two syllables. _____ _____

2. It has a double consonant in its spelling. _____

3. The long e sound in this word is spelled *ie*. _____

4. The word *tire* is part of its spelling. _____

5. It ends with *tion*. _____

6. It begins with the *con-* prefix. _____

7. It ends with a long e sound spelled *y*. _____

8. They begin with the *com-* prefix.

_____ _____

Write the list words with three syllables. Draw lines between the syllables.

9. _____   **12.** _____

10. _____   **13.** _____

11. _____   **14.** _____

Change one letter. Write a list word.

15. field _____   **17.** vocation _____

16. fax _____   **18.** contrast _____

Write the list words that come first and last in alphabetical order.

19. _____

20. _____

⒞ Build Your Skills

Language Tutor

Add an apostrophe and *s* ('*s*) to a singular word to make it show ownership or possession.

the benefits of the company ....the company's benefits
the vacation of Lucy...........................Lucy's vacation
the contract of the union...................the union's contract

Rewrite each group of words. Use 's to show ownership.

1. the book of the library _____

2. the pay of the worker _____

3. the yield of the paycheck _____

4. the picnic of the company _____

5. the salary of Aaron _____

6. the blade of the saw _____

7. the rules of the meeting _____

8. the screen of the computer _____

9. the uniform of the waitress _____

10. the problem of the manager _____

Copy each sentence. Make the word in parentheses show ownership or possession.

11. The (employee) health plan paid the doctor.

_____

12. The (contract) meaning should be clear.

_____

13. Do not shut off the (machine) power.

_____

14. Did you comply with your (supervisor) request?

_____

15. (Mary) goal is to get a better job.

_____

Score: ⟋ 15

Ⓓ Proofread and Write

Donna Lamont received this memo on her first day at work. The memo has four spelling mistakes.
Cross out the misspelled words. Write the words correctly above them.

MEMO

To: Donna Lamont

From: Diana Cole, Personnel Manager

RE: Welcome to Ace Tools

Welcome to the conpany! The attached page summarizes your hourly rate and the anual amount of paid vacasion you will receive. It also explains your health and retirement benefits. In order to compley with the tax law, please fill out the form I gave you last week. If you have any questions, please contact my assistant, Stu Wing. We look forward to having you with us.

Writing Portfolio

Imagine that you are Donna. Write a memo to the personnel manager. Use your own paper. You might ask some questions or just tell her you are looking forward to working for Ace Tools. Proofread your memo carefully and correct any mistakes. Make a clean copy and put it in your writing portfolio.

Getting Ahead in Your Job

Ⓐ Check the Meaning

Read the paragraph below. Think about the meaning of the words in bold type.

Once you get a job, you need to keep it. Even better, you will want to advance to a higher position in the company. **Advancement** or **promotion** requires plenty of hard work. You must work to **improve** your job skills if you hope to turn a job into a **career**, or your life's work. Try to **establish** good work habits and show how willing you are to **develop** your skills. It is also important to have **excellent** speaking and writing skills. These will help you **explain** yourself and understand others. Study the **review** of your work that your supervisor gives you. Work to earn a **superior** rating so that people will see what a good job you are doing.

Write each word in bold type next to its meaning. Check your answers in the Mini-Dictionary.

_____ **1.** a judgment of someone's work

_____ **2.** to make happen little by little

_____ **3.** better than all others

_____ **4.** of very high quality

_____ **5.** to get better or make better

_____ **6.** to set up or create

_____ **7.** to make clear and understandable

_____ **8.** the condition of going above and beyond others

_____ **9.** movement to a better or higher job or rank

_____ **10.** the work one does for life

Score: 10

B Study the Spelling

Word List

| superior | establish | excellent | advancement | develop |
| improve | review | explain | career | promotion |

Write a list word or words for each clue.

1. It comes from the word *advance*. _____

2. It is made from the prefix *re-* and the word *view*. _____

3. It contains the word *super*. _____

4. It ends with *tion*. _____

5. The word *improvement* comes from this word. _____

6. It contains the word *plain*. _____

7. They begin with the prefix *ex-*. _____ _____

8. They end with *ent*. _____ _____

One word in each group is misspelled. Circle the misspelled word. Write it correctly.

9. _____   carear   advancement   superior

10. _____   promotion   establesh   improve

11. _____   explain   excellant   review

Add the missing letters. Then write the words.

12. a___van___ ___ment _____

13. d___vel___p _____

14. expl___ ___n _____

15. impr___v___ _____

Write the three words that begin with *e* in alphabetical order.

16. _____

17. _____

18. _____

© Build Your Skills

Language Tutor

A prefix is a word part at the beginning of a word. A prefix adds meaning to the word.

re- + view = review   pro- + motion = promotion

ex- + plain = explain   dis- + like = dislike

Add the prefixes to each word. Write the new words.

1. re- + new = _____

2. ex- + claim = _____

3. pro- + long = _____

4. re- + appear = _____

5. re- + count = _____

6. dis- + appear = _____

7. ex- + press = _____

8. pro- + claim = _____

9. dis- + please = _____

10. dis- + color = _____

11. pro- + pose = _____

12. re- + fill = _____

13. ex- + cite = _____

14. re- + build = _____

15. dis- + like = _____

16. re- + wind = _____

Copy each sentence. Replace the underlined words with one of the words you wrote for numbers 1–16.

17. The comet will <u>appear</u> <u>again</u> in 2010.

_____

18. We <u>do</u> <u>not</u> <u>like</u> the changes you made.

_____

19. The pastor promised to <u>build</u> the church <u>again</u>.

_____

20. Sally will <u>not</u> <u>please</u> her parents if she moves far away.

_____

Score: /20

Ⓓ Proofread and Write

Jackie worked with her manager to write a job plan. If Jackie follows the plan, she will get a raise in her pay in six months. The plan has four spelling mistakes. Cross out the misspelled words. Write the words correctly above them.

JOB PLAN

1. Ask the crew leader to explain anything you do not understand.

2. Establash a habit of getting to work on time.

3. Watch how Sue helps customers. She does an excelent job.

4. Find one good way to improve the way we fill orders.

5. Develope a way to review your work at the end of the day.

6. Sign up for the courses the company offers for the advancment of your career.

Writing Portfolio

On another piece of paper, write a job plan for the job you have or the job you would like to have. Use at least four list words.

Proofread your job plan carefully and correct any mistakes. Then make a clean copy and put it in your writing portfolio.

Keeping Up on the Job

(A) Check the Meaning

Read the paragraph below. Think about the meaning of the words in bold type.

Modern **science** brings many changes to the office and the shop. Today's office worker must learn the newest **computer** software and the latest operating **system**. The **modem**, which can change sound to pictures, has changed how workers communicate. Some jobs now require workers to learn to use complicated **electric** machines, such as the high-speed stitching machines. The **materials** used in today's products are stronger and more costly. The **machinery** needed for such work has become very difficult to repair. Only an expert should **attempt** such a task. Workers must **adjust** by learning how to use new **tools**. The successful worker never stops learning.

Write each word in bold type next to its meaning. Check your answers in the Mini-Dictionary.

_____ **1.** to change in order to meet new situations

_____ **2.** a device that can process and store information

_____ **3.** an organized way of getting something done

_____ **4.** knowledge of the physical world gathered through experiments

_____ **5.** a device that changes data from one form to another

_____ **6.** powered by a type of energy sent through wires

_____ **7.** to try

_____ **8.** machines in general

_____ **9.** items used to accomplish a task

_____ **10.** things from which other things are made

B Study the Spelling

Word List

science	tool	materials	electric	computer
attempt	machinery	modem	system	adjust

Write the list words with two syllables. Say each word slowly and draw a line between the syllables.

1. _____

2. _____

3. _____

4. _____

5. _____

Write the list word that fits each clue.

6. You can find the word *just* in this word. _____

7. It ends with *tric*. _____

8. It rhymes with *fool*. _____

9. It ends with *er*. _____

10. It is formed from the word *machine*. _____

11. It has a double consonant. _____

12. It begins like *most* and ends like *gem*. _____

Write the three list words that come first in alphabetical order.

13. _____

14. _____

15. _____

Add the missing letters. Then write the word.

16. s___st___m _____

17. a___ju___t _____

18. s___i___nce _____

19. mo___ ___m _____

20. ma___eri___ls _____

21. at___em___t _____

22. c___mput___r _____

23. elect___ ___c _____

24. ma___hin___ry _____

C Build Your Skills

Language Tutor

Add just an apostrophe (') to plural words that end in *s* to make them show ownership or possession.

the uses for the tools ....the tool<u>s</u>' uses
the pictures of the runners.................the runner<u>s</u>' pictures
the union of the workers ....the worker<u>s</u>' union

Rewrite each phrase. Make the underlined word show ownership or possession. The first one has been done for you.

1. the entrance for the new <u>students</u>   <u>the new students' entrance</u>

2. the prizes of the <u>winners</u> _____

3. the health benefits for the <u>workers</u> _____

4. a lounge for the <u>teachers</u> _____

5. the vegetable market of the <u>farmers</u> _____

6. the corral for the wild <u>horses</u> _____

7. rules for the machine <u>operators</u> _____

8. the uniforms of the registered <u>nurses</u> _____

9. orders of the <u>customers</u> _____

10. the meeting of the <u>officers</u> _____

11. the teeth of the <u>wolves</u> _____

12. the keys of the <u>guards</u> _____

Copy each sentence. Make the word in parentheses show ownership or possession.

13. Four of the (clerks) reviews earned a superior rating.

_____

14. Lana studied the (flight attendants) manual all day.

_____

15. Jade will explain the benefits of joining the (employees) credit union.

_____

Ⓓ Proofread and Write

The following set of directions for a new machine has four spelling mistakes. Cross out the misspelled words. Write the words correctly above them.

OPERATOR'S MANUAL

Steps for starting the new X4-2 computer system.

1. If necessary, adjust the speed setting by turning the dial slightly to the left. Use the tool provided with the kit.

2. If the dial sticks, do not attemt to force it open.

3. Turn off the electric power and connect your modam to the proper outlet.

4. Do not place this unit near magnetic materiels.

5. You now have the finest program modern sience has produced.

Writing Portfolio

On another piece of paper, write some steps for using or repairing a machine. It can be a machine you use at work or at home. Use at least four list words.

Proofread your steps carefully and correct any mistakes. Then make a clean copy and put it in your writing portfolio.

12 Getting a Job

Ⓐ Check the Meaning

Read the paragraph below. Think about the meaning of the words in bold type.

Jen Roberts likes people, so she decided to look for a job in a **retail** business, like a store or shop. First, she contacted an employment office. She chose an **agency** that worked closely with local store owners and other **merchants**. The agency knew what kinds of people the merchants wanted to **employ**, the **qualities** the workers needed to have, and the **duties** they would perform. At the agency, Jen got **advice** on how to **prepare** a summary of her skills and work history. Her advisor also helped Jen **determine** how to present herself to the store manager. It was important that she show how **earnest** she was about getting the job and doing it well.

Write each word in bold type next to its meaning. Check your answers in the Mini-Dictionary.

_____ **1.** sincere; serious

_____ **2.** people who sell goods

_____ **3.** a business or group formed to meet a goal

_____ **4.** to decide

_____ **5.** information about how to solve a problem

_____ **6.** to hire

_____ **7.** tasks that are part of a job

_____ **8.** to make ready

_____ **9.** traits or abilities

_____ **10.** selling to the public

Score: /10

B Study the Spelling

Word List

employ	determine	earnest	merchant	qualities
prepare	retail	advice	agency	duties

Write the list word that fits each clue.

1. It rhymes with *fail*. _____

2. It begins with the long a sound you hear in *age* and has three syllables.

_____

3. It begins like *preview* and ends like *care*. _____

4. It begins like *detail* and ends like *examine*. _____

5. The word *employment* comes from this. _____

6. It is the plural of *quality*. _____

7. This is what an advisor gives. _____

8. It has the word *earn* in its spelling. _____

Write the list words with two syllables. Draw a line between the syllables.

9. _____   **13.** _____

10. _____   **14.** _____

11. _____   **15.** _____

12. _____

Form a list word by adding letters from the first column to letters in the second column. Write the list word.

ear	chant	**16.** _____
ad	ploy	**17.** _____
em	vice	**18.** _____
mer	nest	**19.** _____
pre	pare	**20.** _____

C Build Your Skills

Language Tutor

Every sentence must end with a punctuation mark.

A *statement* ends with a period.
> Elena wants a job selling clothes.

A *question* ends with a question mark.
> What is the best way to look for a job?

An *exclamation* of strong feeling ends with an exclamation point.
> I got the job!

Write the correct punctuation mark at the end of each sentence.

1. The store is closed today__

2. Does she own this retail shop__

3. Kate must get ready for work__

4. What a great idea__

5. Ed has the qualities needed for the job__

6. Are you willing to work nights__

7. Jim got help at the agency__

8. Does that company employ welders__

9. What good news I have__

10. Where is the employment office__

Copy each sentence. Add the correct punctuation.

11. This is the most popular store in town

_____

12. When is the best time to apply

_____

13. Come quickly, the store manager is on the phone

_____

14. I can start work next week

_____

D Proofread and Write

Bud was going to meet with a store manager about a job. To get ready, he wrote out some questions the manager might ask him. He also wrote his answers. He made four spelling mistakes and two punctuation mistakes. Cross out the misspelled words and punctuation mistakes. Write the words and punctuation correctly above them.

Questions and Answers

Question: Why do you want to work in retale sales?

Answer: I like meeting people and helping them

determine what to buy?

Question: What have you done to prepare for this

work?

Answer: I worked for a merchent last year. The dutyes

were very much the same.

Question: Why should I employ you.

Answer: I have the qualities you need. I will also be an

ernest worker and help your sales.

Writing Portfolio

Make a list of questions a possible employer might ask you. Use your own paper. Then write your answers to the questions. Use at least four list words. Be sure to use the correct punctuation at the end of each sentence.

Proofread your list of questions carefully and correct any mistakes. Then make a clean copy and put it in your writing portfolio.

Unit 3 Review

Finish the Meaning

Fill in the circle next to the word that best completes each sentence.

1. Sandy will no longer be able to work. She is glad she has a good _____ plan.

   (A) promotion (C) vacation
   (B) retirement (D) advancement

2. Kim got a raise this year. It will increase her weekly _____ by $25.

   (A) qualities (C) review
   (B) system (D) salary

3. The Safety Board just made some strict new rules. We will make every effort to _____ with them.

   (A) comply (C) yield
   (B) employ (D) develop

4. I am not sure I understand the directions. Could you _____ them again, please?

   (A) explain (C) improve
   (B) determine (D) adjust

5. Before you get your first paycheck, you should fill out a(n) _____ form.

   (A) retirement (C) tax
   (B) electric (D) retail

6. Steve is looking for a new job. He will go to a(n) _____ for help.

   (A) vacation (C) modem
   (B) contract (D) agency

7. Pam works at the coffee shop. Her _____ are washing dishes and cleaning tables.

   (A) duties (C) materials
   (B) tools (D) qualities

8. If you want to work in this office, you must know how to use a(n) _____.

   (A) advice (C) agency
   (B) computer (D) vacation

9. Jan arrived early on her first day at her new job. She wants to _____ good work habits.

   (A) cause (C) establish
   (B) consult (D) absorb

10. This business has many new products. It tries to _____ fresh ideas.

    (A) irritate (C) comply
    (B) adjust (D) develop

11. Too many parts were getting lost. A _____ was needed to keep track of them.

    (A) system (C) prescription
    (B) salary (D) promotion

12. Jim did not know what to do. He needed _____ from someone.

    (A) qualities (C) advice
    (B) breath (D) merchandise

Check the Spelling

Fill in the circle next to the word that is spelled correctly and best completes each sentence.

13. Every January Rima gets her _____ review.

(A) annual   (C) anuel
(B) anual   (D) annule

14. Read your _____ carefully before you sign it.

(A) contrakt   (C) contract
(B) contract   (D) kontrakt

15. All the _____ hope sales will be up this year.

(A) murchants   (C) merchents
(B) merchants   (D) merrchants

16. My goal this year is to get a _____ review.

(A) supirior   (C) sooperior
(B) superior   (D) superiur

17. That cake is _____! May I have the recipe?

(A) egscellent   (C) excelent
(B) excellant   (D) excellent

18. Taking classes at night is going to help my _____.

(A) carear   (C) career
(B) cireer   (D) cerear

19. You must _____ carefully for the job interview.

(A) prepar   (C) prepare
(B) prapare   (D) preparre

20. My grandfather worked for the same _____ all his life.

(A) company   (C) companie
(B) cumpanu   (D) compuny

21. Math and _____ were my favorite subjects in school.

(A) sience   (C) science
(B) sciense   (D) siense

22. Always wear heavy boots when working with _____.

(A) machinery   (C) machenery
(B) muchinery   (D) machinerie

23. If you want a good review, _____ to do your best at all times.

(A) attembt   (C) atempt
(B) attemt   (D) attempt

24. Vacation time is probably our best _____.

(A) benafit   (C) banefit
(B) benefit   (D) binafit

STOP

Score: _____ / 24

13 Days and Months

Ⓐ Check the Meaning

Read the paragraph below. Think about the meaning of the words in bold type.

Suppose your new boss told you to start work on **Monday** morning, **February** 8. Would you mark that day on a calendar? A calendar divides time into years, weeks, months, and days. A year has twelve months. We call the first month **January**, the next month February, and so on. These words name a definite period of time, so if school begins on **September** 5, we know when to be there. Time is also divided into weeks and days. A week has seven days. The week begins on **Sunday** and ends on **Saturday**. These two days are often called the weekend. We call the other days weekdays. They follow Sunday in this order: Monday, **Tuesday**, **Wednesday**, **Thursday**, and **Friday**.

Write each word in bold type next to its meaning. Check your answers in the Mini-Dictionary.

_____ **1.** the last day of the week

_____ **2.** the first day of the week

_____ **3.** the first weekday

_____ **4.** the first month of the year

_____ **5.** the last weekday

_____ **6.** the month when school usually starts

_____ **7.** the second weekday

_____ **8.** the day after Tuesday

_____ **9.** the second month of the year

_____ **10.** the day before Friday

Score: ____ / 10

B Study the Spelling

Word List

Sunday	Tuesday	Thursday	Saturday	February
Monday	Wednesday	Friday	January	September

Write the list word or words for each clue.

1. These two days of the week begin with a capital *S*.

_____ _____

2. These days of the week begin with a capital *T*.

_____ _____

3. This day has two *d*'s in its spelling. _____

4. This day has three syllables in its name. _____

5. The names of these two months end with *ary*.

_____ _____

6. This month ends with *ber*. _____

7. This day has the word *sun* in its spelling. _____

8. This day comes first in alphabetical order. _____

9. This day comes last in alphabetical order. _____

Add the missing letters. Write the list word.

10. We___ne___day

_____

11. T___e___day

_____

12. F___ ___day

_____

13. M___ ___day

_____

14. Feb___ ___ary

_____

15. ___ at___rday

_____

One word in each group is misspelled. Circle the misspelled word. Write it correctly.

16. Saturday   Febuary   Tuesday   _____

17. Munday   Thursday   September   _____

18. Sunday   Friday   Wensday   _____

Score: ◻ / 18

Lesson 13: Days and Months   67

ⓒ Build Your Skills

Language Tutor

An abbreviation is a short way of writing a word. Many abbreviations begin with a capital letter and end with a period.

Days of the Week:

Sun.	Sunday
Mon.	Monday
Tues.	Tuesday
Wed.	Wednesday
Thurs.	Thursday
Fri.	Friday
Sat.	Saturday

Months of the Year:

Jan.	January
Feb.	February
Mar.	March
Apr.	April
Aug.	August
Sept.	September
Oct.	October
Nov.	November
Dec.	December

Words in Addresses:

St.	Street
Rd.	Road
Ave.	Avenue
Blvd.	Boulevard
N.	North
E.	East
W.	West
S.	South

Write these dates and addresses using abbreviations.

1. 354 North Adams Street

_____

2. Saturday, August 24, 1997

_____

3. 66 South Lincoln Boulevard

_____

4. Wednesday, February 4, 1998

_____

5. 498 East Madison Avenue

_____

6. Thursday, December 11, 1997

_____

7. 88 North 22nd Street

_____

8. Sunday, February 23, 1997

_____

Write these abbreviations in words.

9. 98 W. Adams St.

_____

10. Thurs., Oct. 1, 1998

_____

11. 2987 N. Walker Ave.

_____

12. Mon., Nov. 30, 1998

_____

13. Sat., Aug. 27, 1994

_____

14. 555 S. Essex Rd.

_____

Score: ⟋ 14

D Proofread and Write

Yolanda made a schedule to help her remember the things she had to do. She made three spelling mistakes. She also made one mistake in an abbreviation. Cross out the misspelled words and abbreviation. Write the words correctly above them.

> ### Week of Sept. 8-14
>
> **Sunday**   see about child care for Fri. night, Febuary 12
>
> **Monday**   meet Beth on Broad St.
>
> **Tuesday**   look for new apartment
>
> **Wenesday**   make cake for party on Thers.
>
> **Thursday**   get ready for trip
>
> **Friday**   pick up Tim after work on E. Adams Blvd.
>
> **Saterday**   buy books for class

Write a schedule for one of your weeks. Use at least four list words and one abbreviation.

_____

_____

_____

_____

_____

_____

_____

Writing Portfolio

Proofread your schedule carefully and correct any mistakes. Then make a clean copy and put it in your writing portfolio.

14 Getting Help

Ⓐ Check the Meaning

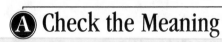

Read the paragraph below. Think about the meaning of the words in bold type.

Last week a fire destroyed a **building** where many people worked. Without jobs for a time, workers needed some **temporary** help. The **government** provided help in several ways. One group that helped was the city's **department** of special services. To get help, the workers had to provide some facts and meet certain **requirements**. Then the city workers made a **decision** on the kind of help they could give and on how long help could **continue**. Besides these **public** or government programs, the **community** had several private sources of help in the crisis. A **church** offered meals. Another charity took care of children while workers looked for jobs.

Write each word in bold type next to its meaning. Check your answers in the Mini-Dictionary.

_____ **1.** a place where many people live together

_____ **2.** part of a large business, government, or organization

_____ **3.** people or system for managing a community, state, or country

_____ **4.** a place where people meet to worship or pray

_____ **5.** to keep on happening

_____ **6.** a structure usually having walls and a roof

_____ **7.** a conclusion or judgment

_____ **8.** things that are needed or demanded

_____ **9.** lasting for a short time

_____ **10.** supported and used by the community; not private

B Study the Spelling

Word List

community	public	government	requirement	building
department	temporary	church	continue	decision

Form a list word by adding letters from the first column to letters from the second column. Write the list word.

com	ernment	**1.**	_____
de	porary	**2.**	_____
con	munity	**3.**	_____
tem	partment	**4.**	_____
gov	tinue	**5.**	_____

Write the list word for each clue.

6. It comes from the word *require*. _____

7. It begins and ends with *ch*. _____

8. It has a double *m* in its spelling. _____

9. It ends with *ary*. _____

10. It comes from the word *govern*. _____

11. It has the word *tin* in its spelling. _____

12. It comes from the word *decide*. _____

Write the list words that end with *ment*. Draw lines between the syllables.

13. _____   **15.** _____

14. _____

Add the missing letters. Write the list word.

16. gov___r___ment _____

17. publ___ ___ _____

18. b___il___ing _____

Ⓒ Build Your Skills

Language Tutor

A suffix is a word part added to the end of a word. A suffix can change the meaning of a word. It can also change how a word is used in a sentence.

Word	+	Suffix	=	New Word
govern		-ment		government
good		-ness		goodness
instruct		-ion		instruction
govern		-or		governor
bake		-er		baker
love		-able		lovable

Note that the final *e* is usually dropped before adding a suffix that begins with a vowel.

Add the suffix to each word. Then write the new word.

1. pay + -able _____

2. excite + -ment _____

3. value + -able _____

4. place + -ment _____

5. manage + -er _____

6. act + -ion _____

7. improve + -ment _____

8. accept + -able _____

9. conduct + -or _____

10. believe + -able _____

Copy each sentence. Add the suffix in parentheses to the underlined word.

11. The owner wanted $2500 for the car, but she would take any <u>reason</u> offer. (able)

_____

12. The doctor said my <u>ill</u> would not last long. (ness)

_____

13. Pedro put on the brakes, but an accident was not <u>avoid</u>. (able)

_____

14. Before you can get a license, your car must pass an <u>inspect</u>. (ion)

_____

15. The batter did not agree with the umpire's <u>judge</u>. (ment)

_____

Score: / 15

D Proofread and Write

The following notice was printed in the newspaper. The notice has four spelling errors. Cross out the misspelled words. Write the words correctly above them.

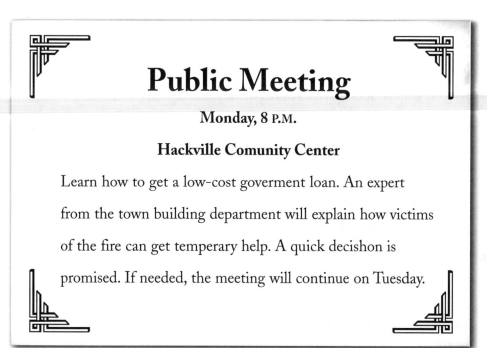

Public Meeting

Monday, 8 P.M.

Hackville Comunity Center

Learn how to get a low-cost goverment loan. An expert

from the town building department will explain how victims

of the fire can get temperary help. A quick decishon is

promised. If needed, the meeting will continue on Tuesday.

Write a notice for a newspaper or bulletin board. Give some information you think might be useful to someone looking for help. Use at least four list words.

_____

_____

_____

_____

_____

_____

_____

Writing Portfolio

Proofread your notice carefully and correct any mistakes. Then make a clean copy and put it in your writing portfolio.

The Holiday Spirit

Ⓐ Check the Meaning

Read the paragraph below. Think about the meaning of the words in bold type.

Like people everywhere, Americans **celebrate** certain **holidays**. The United States has many kinds of people, so it has many kinds of holidays. Some mark **historic** events, such as the Fourth of July, the country's **official** birthday. On these days, people **assemble** at parades and parties. Other holidays, such as **Memorial Day**, are quieter. We **dedicate** that day to people who died in war. **Halloween** is not an official holiday, but many children like it. On this **occasion** they dress in masks and costumes. Some holidays are celebrated at the end of summer, such as Rosh Hashanah, the Jewish New Year. Others are celebrated in winter, including Kwanza, an African-American festival, and **Christmas**, an important Christian feast day.

Write each word in bold type next to its meaning. Check your answers in the Mini-Dictionary.

_____ **1.** to set apart for a special use

_____ **2.** important in history

_____ **3.** to gather together

_____ **4.** to mark in a special way

_____ **5.** days set aside to recall an important event

_____ **6.** a day to remember people who died in war

_____ **7.** a Christian feast day

_____ **8.** a day children dress up in masks

_____ **9.** approved by proper authorities; proper

_____ **10.** any special event or time

Score: _____ /10

B Study the Spelling

Word List

official	dedicate	assemble	Christmas	holidays
occasion	Memorial Day	celebrate	Halloween	historic

Write the list word or words for each clue.

1. It has a double *c* and one *s* in its spelling. _____

2. It comes from the word *history*. _____

3. It has a double *s* and two *e*'s in its spelling. _____

4. It comes from the word *memory*. _____

5. It has a double *l* and a double *e* in its spelling. _____

6. It is two words. _____

7. It has two syllables and is a holiday. _____

8. They end with *ate*. _____ _____

Write the list words that begin with capital letters. Underline the capital letters.

9. _____   **11.** _____

10. _____

Add the missing letters. Write the list word.

12. of___i___ial _____   **15.** hol___da___s _____

13. o___ca___ion _____   **16.** ___hristm___s _____

14. as___emb___e _____   **17.** cel___br___te _____

Form a list word by adding letters from the first column to letters from the second column. Write the list word.

18. cele   cate   _____

19. dedi   ial   _____

20. offic   brate   _____

Score: /20

C Build Your Skills

Language Tutor

Nouns name persons, places, things, or ideas. A proper noun names a particular person, place, thing, or idea. Holidays, months, and days of the week are proper nouns. A proper noun always begins with a capital letter.

Common Noun	Proper Noun
tomorrow	Memorial Day
people	Dr. Luis Rivera
place	Kansas City
thing	Atlantic Ocean
group	Sierra Club

Copy these sentences. Begin each proper noun with a capital letter.

1. I will meet dr. chin at the corner of lake street and columbus avenue.

   _____

2. The christmas party was held in the lawrence hillman library.

   _____

3. On tuesday, mr. conners flew to ireland on shamrock airlines.

   _____

4. sue will be in los angeles for new year's eve.

   _____

5. The bakersfield garden club meets every wednesday.

   _____

6. We will have a costume party to celebrate halloween.

   _____

7. The attack on fort williams was led by captain logan.

   _____

8. Few passengers survived the sinking of the ocean liner *titanic*.

   _____

9. You must change to another bus in dallas, texas.

   _____

10. The meeting with senator davis was held on tuesday.

    _____

Score: / 10

D Proofread and Write

Jake sent this invitation to several friends. His invitation has four spelling mistakes. Cross out the misspelled words. Write the words correctly above them.

354 High Street

Springfield, VA 22150

May 12, 1997

Dear Alf and Ira,

I would like you to come to my house for a Memoreal Day picnic. Since this is an official holiday, I hope you have the day off and can join several friends I am having over. I haven't seen you since last Chrismas, or was it Halloween? I love an occassion when we can all get together.

This year, I am having an all-day picnic. Everyone is bringing one kind of food. Let me know what you would like to bring. We also have something special to cellebrate.

My son Wayne was married last month. You will meet his new wife if you come. Let me know by next week.

Best wishes,

Jake

Writing Portfolio

Write a letter inviting someone to share a special day with you. Use your own paper. Use at least four list words.

Proofread your letter carefully and correct any mistakes. Then make a clean copy and put it in your writing portfolio.

16 Making an Emergency Call

Ⓐ Check the Meaning

Read the paragraph below. Think about the meaning of the words in bold type.

To get help in an **emergency**, you may need to call a special telephone number. Most phone books **include** a list of important numbers on the first page. A **hotel** may list these numbers in a special **booklet** kept near the phone. Many places use 911 for emergencies because it is easy to remember and everyone will **recognize** it. When calling, try to stay calm, **regardless** of the danger, even though this may be **difficult**. The person who answers the phone will **interview** you and ask several questions. Give **complete** information: what happened, where you are, and what the emergency is. Stay on the line until you get a **signal** to hang up or to take a certain action.

Write each word in bold type next to its meaning. Check your answers in the Mini-Dictionary.

_____ **1.** to contain, along with other things

_____ **2.** a sign or word that tells you something

_____ **3.** a place that rents rooms

_____ **4.** without regard or consideration

_____ **5.** a sudden event that needs quick action

_____ **6.** total; everything that is needed

_____ **7.** a small book

_____ **8.** not easy; hard

_____ **9.** to know something when you see it

_____ **10.** to ask questions of

B Study the Spelling

Word List

include	signal	interview	recognize	hotel
regardless	emergency	difficult	booklet	complete

Write the list word or words for each clue.

1. It has the suffix *-less.* _____

2. It contains the word *sign.* _____

3. It is made from the word *book* and the suffix *-let.* _____

4. The prefix *inter-* is added to the word *view.* _____

5. It begins with the prefix *com-.* _____

6. It contains four syllables. _____

7. It ends with *ize.* _____

8. It rhymes with *motel.* _____

Write the list words with two syllables. Draw a line between the two syllables.

9. _____

10. _____

11. _____

12. _____

13. _____

Combine the underlined parts of each pair of words. Write a list word.

14. <u>inter</u>fere   pre<u>view</u> _____

15. <u>in</u>tend   ex<u>clude</u> _____

16. dis<u>regard</u>   un<u>less</u> _____

One word in each group is misspelled. Circle the misspelled word. Write it correctly.

17. dificult   booklet   complete _____

18. include   recognize   emergancy _____

C Build Your Skills

Language Tutor

Words are placed in the dictionary in alphabetical order. Words beginning with *a* come before words that begin with *b* and so on. If the first letters are the same, compare the next letters. Continue until you come to letters that are different.

a b c d e f g h i j k l m n o p q r s t u v w x y z

The words in each list are in alphabetical order.

booklet	recognize	include
complete	regardless	interest
difficult	signal	interview

Write each group of words in alphabetical order.

1. hotel emergency complete

_____

_____

_____

2. signal telephone money

_____

_____

_____

3. explain examine factory

_____

_____

_____

4. director church comply

_____

_____

_____

5. annual appeal total

_____

_____

_____

6. dentist permit percent

_____

_____

_____

7. avenue apartment garage

_____

_____

_____

8. knowledge nobody knee

_____

_____

_____

Score: /8

Ⓓ Proofread and Write

Sam let Enrique use his apartment while he was away. Sam left the following note for Enrique. His note has four spelling mistakes. Cross out the misspelled words. Write the words correctly above them.

Enrique,

I am staying at a hotel in El Paso. The phone number is 555-6789. Call me in an emurgency regardles of the time. If you get a busy signal, leave a message at the desk. The other numbers you need are in the booklet near the phone. The list will include the number of a doctor and the police. I left a compleate set of extra keys with the man next door. I described you to him, so he will recagnize you when he sees you. Enjoy the apartment.

Sam

Writing Portfolio

On another piece of paper, write a note to someone who will be staying in your home. Tell the person the things you think he or she should know. Use at least four list words.

Proofread your note carefully and correct any mistakes. Make a clean copy and put it in your writing portfolio.

Unit 4 Review

Finish the Meaning

Fill in the circle next to the word that best completes each sentence.

1. Ramon will work a double shift on Friday. The next day is _____, so he has the day off.

   (A) Sunday   (C) Monday
   (B) Saturday   (D) Wednesday

2. Before baking a cake, _____ everything you will need.

   (A) recommend   (C) cause
   (B) employ   (D) assemble

3. Sandy needs _____ housing while she looks for a new place to live.

   (A) dangerous   (C) temporary
   (B) historic   (D) average

4. The reporter wanted to _____ everyone.

   (A) interview   (C) deceive
   (B) neglect   (D) adjust

5. After the race, will you _____ to run every day?

   (A) continue   (C) increase
   (B) include   (D) charge

6. Mark is in sales and Sally is in housekeeping. Which _____ do you work for?

   (A) qualities   (C) department
   (B) opportunity   (D) percent

7. Craig's birthday is next week. He plans to _____ with his friends.

   (A) respond   (C) improve
   (B) signal   (D) celebrate

8. Kalynn loves to wear costumes. _____ is her favorite day of the year.

   (A) Memorial Day   (C) Christmas
   (B) Halloween   (D) Tuesday

9. Answer all the questions on the form. We will only process applications that are _____.

   (A) excellent   (C) complete
   (B) duties   (D) enormous

10. The park is open to everyone. It serves the entire _____.

    (A) bank   (C) career
    (B) kitchen   (D) community

11. You must wear a hard hat. They are one of the _____ in this plant.

    (A) occasions   (C) requirements
    (B) tools   (D) departments

12. I like Christmas best of all. What are your favorite _____?

    (A) holidays   (C) companies
    (B) agencies   (D) environments

GO ON

Check the Spelling

Fill in the circle next to the word that is spelled correctly and best completes each sentence.

13. The second month is _____. It is also the shortest month of the year.

- (A) Febuary
- (B) Febuery
- (C) February
- (D) Febroary

14. In the United States, we vote for our leaders. This is our democratic form of _____.

- (A) goverment
- (B) government
- (C) guvernment
- (D) govornment

15. I hope we have an _____ to meet again soon.

- (A) occasion
- (B) occaision
- (C) ocasion
- (D) occaision

16. Always keep a first-aid kit ready for an _____.

- (A) emurgency
- (B) emergency
- (C) emurgincy
- (D) emergincy

17. The company's health plan is described in the _____.

- (A) buklet
- (B) booklette
- (C) buklette
- (D) booklet

18. Most students chose the wrong answer. It was a _____ problem.

- (A) dificult
- (B) diffacult
- (C) difficult
- (D) difacult

19. Will you stay in a _____ or with friends?

- (A) hotelle
- (B) hotel
- (C) houtel
- (D) hottel

20. Kirk has a dentist appointment next _____.

- (A) Thursday
- (B) Thersday
- (C) Thursdey
- (D) Thersdey

21. The _____ start of winter is December 22.

- (A) offishel
- (B) oficial
- (C) offeshul
- (D) official

22. The school is the first _____ on the right.

- (A) bilding
- (B) building
- (C) biulding
- (D) buillding

23. We will _____ the park to the former mayor.

- (A) deadicate
- (B) dedikate
- (C) dedicate
- (D) deadikate

24. A _____ school is open to anyone.

- (A) publick
- (B) publik
- (C) public
- (D) pablic

STOP

17 The Roots of Democracy

A Check the Meaning

Read the paragraph below. Think about the meaning of the words in bold type.

The United States began as small **settlements**. Many people came from England in search of **religious** freedom. As years passed, these settlers felt less and less like British subjects. They had no voice in the laws and taxes. By 1775 the desire for **liberty** led to a **revolution**. After years of fighting, the British were finally defeated. The **patriots** held a **convention** to make a new government. At first they wanted to remain as thirteen separate states. This plan did not work. In 1789 they drew up a **document** that became our **constitution**. It promised a **democratic** form of government. Unlike British rule, it would be **representative** of the wishes of the people.

Write each word in bold type next to its meaning. Check your answers in the Mini-Dictionary.

_____ **1.** having to do with one's belief in God

_____ **2.** a type of government in which power belongs to the people

_____ **3.** a statement of the basic plan for a government

_____ **4.** being a good example of the ideas or beliefs of others

_____ **5.** freedom from the control of others

_____ **6.** those loyal to a country

_____ **7.** an official paper

_____ **8.** a meeting for a definite purpose

_____ **9.** an uprising against one's government

_____ **10.** a small, new community

B Study the Spelling

Word List

convention	representative	liberty	constitution	religious
democratic	document	revolution	patriot	settlement

Write the list word that is formed from each of these words.

1. religion _____

2. revolve _____

3. settle _____

4. represent _____

5. convene _____

6. democracy _____

Write the word or words from the list for each clue.

7. It ends with the suffix *-ment*. _____

8. They begin with *con* and end with *tion*. _____

_____

9. It has five syllables. _____

10. It rhymes with *property*. _____

Write the list words with three syllables. Draw a line between the syllables.

11. _____

12. _____

13. _____

14. _____

15. _____

16. _____

Add the missing letters. Write the list word.

17. const___t___tion _____

18. rev___l___tion _____

19. rel___gi___us _____

20. doc___m___nt _____

C Build Your Skills

Language Tutor

A sentence begins with a capital letter and ends with a period, a question mark, or an exclamation point.

Statement:	The patriots fought for liberty.
Question:	When did the American Revolution take place?
Exclamation:	Here they come!

Copy each sentence. Add capital letters and end punctuation.

1. did you study about the Boston Tea Party

_____

2. one famous patriot was named Samuel Adams

_____

3. help is on the way

_____

4. where was the U.S. Constitution written

_____

5. the convention was held in Philadelphia

_____

6. is that document important

_____

7. we enjoy religious freedom in this country

_____

8. I forgot we were having a history test today

_____

9. she is our representative in Washington

_____

10. this is a democratic nation

_____

11. where did you put that document

_____

12. never stop fighting for your ideas

_____

Score: / 12

D Proofread and Write

Bruce got the following handbill in the mail. It has three spelling mistakes. The writer also forgot how to begin and end one sentence. Cross out the misspelled words. Write the correct spellings above them. Add the missing capital letter and end punctuation.

Wake Up, America!!!

Do you believe in a demacratic government?

Do you want a represenative who stands up for liberty?

Do you want to save the rights promised by the Constitution?

if you do, then vote for Steve Wells

Keep the spirit of revolution alive!

Put a patroit in Congress!

Writing Portfolio

Write a handbill that asks the reader to support a candidate or a law. Use your own paper. Include at least five list words and one question.

Proofread your handbill carefully and correct any mistakes. Then make a clean copy and put it in your writing portfolio.

18 Reducing Waste

(A) Check the Meaning

Read the paragraph below. Think about the meaning of the words in bold type.

You may have heard the **slogan**, "Reduce, Reuse, Recycle." Some **local** laws in towns or villages make people **recycle** papers, glass, and other waste. These towns **forbid** throwing away such items. Instead, people must return them so they can be reused. Since this is a law, **legal** action can be taken against those not in **compliance** with this rule. Those who **advocate** such laws see them as a way of saving our **natural** resources. If we can **regulate** the waste that is burned or buried, the **habitat** of wildlife is also protected. Without a proper place to live, some types of wildlife will disappear forever. This would be a great loss. The wildlife could not be replaced.

Write each word in bold type next to its meaning. Check your answers in the Mini-Dictionary.

_____ **1.** the place where a plant or animal normally lives or grows

_____ **2.** a saying or phrase used to promote an idea

_____ **3.** to order someone not to do something

_____ **4.** provided by nature; not made by people

_____ **5.** to recommend or urge

_____ **6.** to control through certain rules

_____ **7.** the act of following someone's rules or wishes

_____ **8.** to return something for use again

_____ **9.** having to do with the law

_____ **10.** having to do with a particular, limited area

Score: / 10

B Study the Spelling

Word List

slogan	natural	recycle	forbid	regulate
compliance	habitat	local	legal	advocate

Write the list word or words for each clue.

1. They end with *ate*.

   _____   _____

2. It comes from the word *comply*. _____

3. It contains the word *habit*. _____

4. They end with *al*.

   _____

   _____

   _____

5. It has the word *cycle* in its spelling. _____

Form a list word by adding letters from the first column to letters from the second column. Write the list word.

le	cal	6. _____
slo	gan	7. _____
for	bid	8. _____
lo	gal	9. _____
nat	ural	10. _____

One word in each group is misspelled. Circle the misspelled word. Write it correctly on the line.

11. complience	habitat	natural	_____
12. advocate	reguate	slogan	_____
13. forebid	legal	local	_____
14. recycle	advacate	compliance	_____

C Build Your Skills

Language Tutor

A prefix is added to the beginning of a word. It changes the meaning of the word. Some prefixes are added to word roots. A word root has meaning, but it usually doesn't stand by itself as a word.

Prefix	Meaning	Word or Root	New Word	Meaning
re-	again	cycle	recycle	to cycle again
il-	not	legal	illegal	not legal
un-	not	natural	unnatural	not natural
pre-	before	historic	prehistoric	before history
com-	together	bine	combine	to bring together

Add a prefix to the word or root. Write the new word and its meaning.

pre- + view =   1. _____ _____

il- + logical =   2. _____ _____

com- + pare =   3. _____ _____

com- + press =   4. _____ _____

un- + usual =   5. _____ _____

re- + view =   6. _____ _____

il- + legal =   7. _____ _____

un- + comfortable = 8. _____ _____

pre- + pare =   9. _____ _____

com- + plete =   10. _____ _____

un- + realistic =   11. _____ _____

re- + placement =   12. _____ _____

D Proofread and Write

The following story appeared in the newspaper. It contained four spelling mistakes. Cross out the misspelled words. Write the correct spellings above them.

New Laws Will Reguate Waste

Two local advacates helped pass a new law. This new law ferbids the burning of trash. People must also recycle all paper and glass. The mayor says she expects full legul compliance by everyone in town. She also says more steps may be needed to regulate other forms of waste.

Write a short newspaper story. Describe a recycling law that has passed or that you would like to see passed. Use at least four list words.

_____

_____

_____

_____

_____

_____

_____

_____

 Writing Portfolio

Proofread your story carefully and correct any mistakes. Then make a clean copy and put it in your writing portfolio.

It's the Law

Ⓐ Check the Meaning

Read the paragraph below. Think about the meaning of the words in bold type.

A **citizen** of this country has certain rights. The police cannot jail someone without a reason. They must **accuse** that person of a crime. If they do not, they must free him. If someone is placed under **arrest**, he has the right to a lawyer. In some cases, the courts will provide one free of charge. In addition, the accused has the right to an **examination** of any **evidence**. Most of all, everyone has the right to a fair trial. At that time all the evidence is weighed. Only then can the law **convict** a citizen of a crime. A judge is in charge of the **court** where the **trial** takes place. He or she must see that **justice** is done. Even if the accused is found guilty, he can **dispute** the result of the trial. He can then take his case to a higher court.

Write each word in bold type next to its meaning. Check your answers in the Mini-Dictionary.

_____ **1.** to hold or capture for breaking a law

_____ **2.** fairness in the eyes of the law

_____ **3.** a close review or study

_____ **4.** a member of a country who has rights and responsibilities

_____ **5.** facts or signs that appear to prove something

_____ **6.** to find or prove to be guilty

_____ **7.** to question or deny the truth of something

_____ **8.** a process for deciding the truth

_____ **9.** to charge someone with doing wrong

_____ **10.** a place where legal matters are decided

B Study the Spelling

Word List

justice	arrest	citizen	convict	accuse
dispute	trial	evidence	examination	court

Write the list word or words for each clue.

1. They have double consonants in their spellings. _____

_____

2. It rhymes with *port* and has just one syllable. _____

3. It has two syllables and ends with *al*. _____

4. It begins with the prefix *dis-*. _____

5. It contains the word *exam*. _____

6. The word *just* is part of its spelling. _____

Write the three list words that begin with *c* in alphabetical order.

7. _____

8. _____

9. _____

Replace the underlined prefix to write a list word.

10. <u>ex</u>cuse _____   12. <u>com</u>pute _____

11. <u>e</u>vict _____   13. <u>pro</u>vidence _____

Write the list words with two or more syllables. Draw lines between the syllables.

14. _____   19. _____

15. _____   20. _____

16. _____   21. _____

17. _____   22. _____

18. _____

Ⓒ Build Your Skills

Language Tutor

Always capitalize a person's name. Capitalize a person's title if the title comes
before the name.

Mr. Charles W. Frazier	Ms. Juanita K. Perez
Mayor Wingert	President Clinton
Uncle Sid	Captain Lester
Dr. Julio Sanders	Dean Robertson

Write each sentence. Capitalize any names and titles.

1. The judge ruled in favor of mr. and mrs. kilpatrick.

_____

2. The court did not convict dr. wells.

_____

3. In court, judge davidson read the charges against ms. blair.

_____

4. Will dr. fishman's case go to trial?

_____

5. We asked senator thompson to give a speech.

_____

6. The judge gave mayor hudson the oath of office.

_____

7. It has been four days since mr. nashawati's arrest.

_____

8. The examination was given by dr. wu.

_____

9. Did ms. larson attend the trial?

_____

10. Our lawyer, mrs. clayton, will help us.

_____

D Proofread and Write

Delia Carter received the following notice in the mail. It has three spelling mistakes and one mistake in capitalization. Cross out the misspelled words. Write the correct spellings above them. Write the correct capital letter above the word that should capitalized.

Cobb County Court

February 21, 1997

Delia Carter

176 Constitution Place

Tampa, FL 33611

Dear Ms. Carter:

You are to report for jury duty on March 6, 1997, at 8:30 A.M. Please report to judge Fisher's court at 44 Main Street. You may be assigned to a trail that takes several days, because the examination of witnesses takes time. Be prepared to stay in court for a week or more. As a citizan, it is your duty to look at the evidence to see that justise is done. Please inform us within ten days if you are unable to report.

Sincerely,

James Meyer

James Meyer

Clerk of the Court

Writing Portfolio

Write a letter to the clerk of the court. Ask to have your jury duty moved to another day because of your job. Use your own paper. Use at least four list words.

Proofread your letter carefully and correct mistakes. Then make a clean copy and put it in your writing portfolio.

20 The Branches of Government

Ⓐ Check the Meaning

Read the paragraph below. Think about the meaning of the words in bold type.

The U.S. government has three main parts. They are sometimes called branches. The law-making branch is the **Congress**. Here the men and women sent by the voters **debate** the issues and pass laws. Often they begin by forming a small **committee**. There they can **discuss** certain topics more fully. They may then decide to **enact** a new law. The courts are another branch. It is this branch that must define the law. It also must **enforce** the laws through fair trials. The third branch is made up of the president and the **cabinet**, a group of advisors. We look to the president for the **defense** of our country. The president also can **veto**, or reject, laws passed by Congress. If the president signs a **treaty** with another country, it must be approved by the Senate, a part of Congress.

Write each word in bold type next to its meaning. Check your answers in the Mini-Dictionary.

_____ **1.** to talk over together

_____ **2.** to argue in a formal way

_____ **3.** a group of advisors to the president

_____ **4.** an agreement between two countries

_____ **5.** to make into a law

_____ **6.** to reject a law passed by Congress

_____ **7.** the law-making branch of the U.S. government

_____ **8.** a group of people selected to do a job or discuss a problem

_____ **9.** to see that laws or rules are followed

_____ **10.** the act of protecting against attack or harm

Score: ⁄ 10

B Study the Spelling

Word List

enact	Congress	defense	cabinet	debate
treaty	veto	discuss	enforce	committee

Write the list word or words for each clue.

1. It has the word *cabin* in it. _____

2. It has three sets of double letters. _____

3. It begins with the *con-* prefix. _____

4. They end with a double *s*.

   _____   _____

5. It has the word *act* in its spelling. _____

6. It has the word *force* in its spelling. _____

7. It has four letters and two syllables. _____

8. It rhymes with *meaty*. _____

9. They have three syllables.

   _____   _____

Add the missing letters. Write a list word.

10. cab___n___t _____

11. com___itte___ _____

12. tre___t___ _____

13. d___b___te _____

14. C___ngr___ss _____

15. d___fen___e _____

One word in each group is misspelled. Circle the misspelled word. Write it correctly.

16. debate   defense   commitee   _____

17. cabinit   enact   discuss   _____

18. defense   treety   Congress   _____

19. discuss   enforse   debate   _____

20. vetoe   Congress   enact   _____

© Build Your Skills

Language Tutor

A common noun is a person, place, thing, or idea. A proper noun names a particular person, place, thing, or idea. A specific part of a country's government is a proper noun. A proper noun always begins with a capital letter.

Common Noun	Proper Noun
congress	the United States Congress
city	Kansas City
ocean	Pacific Ocean
organization	United Nations
building	Yankee Stadium

Write each of these sentences. Capitalize the proper nouns.

1. My aunt Frieda lives in duluth, minnesota.

_____

2. I have never seen lake tahoe.

_____

3. Mrs. Marquez is from peru, but her friend is from mexico.

_____

4. The meeting was held in the jones arena.

_____

5. Will president clinton attend the conference?

_____

6. I heard that death valley is the hottest spot in the united states.

_____

7. Her case went to the U.S. supreme court.

_____

8. Meet me at maple street near the kennedy library.

_____

9. We drive south as far as crater lake.

_____

10. Is niagara falls in new york?

Score: / 10

Ⓓ Proofread and Write

Kevin Whitman wrote this letter to his representative in Congress. It contains three spelling mistakes. He also forgot to capitalize one proper noun. Cross out the misspelled words. Write the correct spellings above them. Write the correct capital letter above the proper noun.

656 Amelia Road

Jefferson City, MO 65109

April 12, 1997

Fred Sherman

House of Representatives

Washington, DC 20515

Dear Representative Sherman:

I am writing to ask you to vote against spending more money on defence. This is the second time Congress will debate this bill. It did not pass the first time. Why keep trying to spend money we do not have? Besides, the comittee did not really discuss this bill thoroughly.

The President has promised to veto any more spending on weapons. He and everyone in his cabnet are against this bill. They say it will hurt the chances for the treaty being discussed in washington. Please vote not to enact this bill.

Sincerely,

Kevin Whitman

Kevin Whitman

Writing Portfolio

Write a letter to your representative in Congress. Use your own paper. Tell your representative what laws you think are needed. Use at least four list words.

Proofread your letter carefully and correct any mistakes. Then make a clean copy. Mail it to your representative or put it in your writing folder.

Unit 5 Review

Finish the Meaning

Fill in the circle next to the word that best completes each sentence.

1. When people elect others to speak for them, their government is called _____.

   (A) official   (C) representative
   (B) average   (D) trustworthy

2. I am sorry, but you cannot park there. The fire laws _____ it.

   (A) forbid   (C) permit
   (B) neglect   (D) cause

3. If you think your bill is not right, call the office to _____ it.

   (A) dispute   (C) recognize
   (B) complain   (D) dedicate

4. If the president does not like a new law, he or she can _____ it.

   (A) increase   (C) yield
   (B) veto   (D) include

5. Your driver's license is an important _____. Keep it in a safe place.

   (A) coupon   (C) booklet
   (B) benefit   (D) document

6. The government does not want us to eat harmful food. It _____ what can be sold in stores.

   (A) regulates   (C) poisons
   (B) refunds   (D) interviews

7. I'm not sure what I should to do about this problem. I will _____ it with the boss.

   (A) compare   (C) assemble
   (B) discuss   (D) refund

8. You may have lived in this country for many years, but you must be a(n) _____ to vote.

   (A) athlete   (C) citizen
   (B) dentist   (D) doctor

9. George Washington fought for our country. He was a great _____.

   (A) signal   (C) document
   (B) occasion   (D) patriot

10. We never throw out our newspapers. We _____ them instead.

    (A) absorb   (C) dedicate
    (B) develop   (D) recycle

11. He may be the thief, but without _____ we cannot prove it.

    (A) prescription   (C) requirement
    (B) evidence   (D) teeth

12. If you plan to run for office, be prepared to _____ the issues.

    (A) debate   (C) deposit
    (B) irritate   (D) chill

GO ON

Check the Spelling

Fill in the circle next to the word that is spelled correctly and best completes each sentence.

13. Americans celebrate their _____ on July 4.

  (A) liberty   (C) libberty
  (B) libertie   (D) libaty

14. It is not _____ to park on this street.

  (A) legel   (C) legle
  (B) leegal   (D) legal

15. The _____ will decide if he broke the law.

  (A) kourt   (C) court
  (B) cort   (D) courte

16. The _____ will allow more open trade between the countries.

  (A) treaty   (C) treatie
  (B) treety   (D) treetie

17. In a _____ system, each person gets one vote.

  (A) demacratic   (C) demokratic
  (B) democratic   (D) demakratik

18. Animals do best in their natural _____.

  (A) habitate   (C) habbitat
  (B) habitat   (D) habittat

19. The prisoner claimed she was denied _____ by the jury.

  (A) justise   (C) justes
  (B) justis   (D) justice

20. The police work to _____ the laws.

  (A) inforce   (C) inforse
  (B) enforse   (D) enforce

21. Because it was a _____ holiday, he did not have to work.

  (A) religious   (C) religes
  (B) raligious   (D) religous

22. To sell this merchandise, we will need a good advertising _____.

  (A) slogun   (C) slogan
  (B) slowgan   (D) sloggan

23. Did she _____ you of forgetting the date?

  (A) acuse   (C) acusse
  (B) accuse   (D) accusse

24. The safety _____ found everything in order.

  (A) comittee   (C) committe
  (B) commitee   (D) committee

STOP

Score: ___/24

21 Plan for Success

A Check the Meaning

Read the paragraph below. Think about the meaning of the words in bold type.

Sometimes, it is a **challenge** to find enough time to work, play, and learn. Planning can help. First, you must **define** your goals. What are you trying to do? Be clear and specific. For **example**, do not just say you want to get an **education**. Decide exactly what you want to learn. Write a **statement** about your goal, such as "I want to pass the math test." Each day, **refer** to your list of goals. Plan what you can do to reach each goal. If you want better grades, study someone who gets good grades. Use that person as a **model**. Do you want to speak well? Learn to use a **dictionary** and **practice** using new words when you talk and write. Don't be afraid of failure. You will only **fail** if you don't set any goals.

Write each word in bold type next to its meaning. Check your answers in the Mini-Dictionary.

_____ **1.** a sample of something

_____ **2.** a sentence that states or says something

_____ **3.** something worthy of being copied

_____ **4.** to describe or explain exactly

_____ **5.** to fall short of a goal; not succeed

_____ **6.** to repeat in order to learn

_____ **7.** a task or goal that is hard to reach

_____ **8.** knowledge or learning that is gained

_____ **9.** a book that gives the meaning, pronunciation, and other information about words

_____ **10.** to check for information or help

B Study the Spelling

Word List

example	define	statement	fail	refer
education	dictionary	practice	model	challenge

Write the list word or words for each clue.

1. It comes from the word *educate*. _____

2. The word *fine* is part of its spelling. _____

3. It adds the suffix -*ment* to the word *state*. _____

4. It ends with *ary*. _____

5. It rhymes with *prefer*. _____

6. It has just one syllable. _____

Write the list words with two syllables. Draw a line between the syllables.

7. _____   **10.** _____

8. _____   **11.** _____

9. _____   **12.** _____

Add the missing letters. Write the list word.

13. examp___ ___   **15.** chal___eng___

_____   _____

14. mod___ ___   **16.** d___f___ne

_____   _____

Write the following words in alphabetical order: *example, refer, education, statement*.

17. _____   **19.** _____

18. _____   **20.** _____

Lesson 21: Plan for Success (103)

C Build Your Skills

Language Tutor

A dictionary tells you how a word is said, or pronounced. It does this by respelling the word using special symbols. These symbols stand for sounds. Unlike letters, these symbols always stand for the same sounds.

Word	Dictionary Respelling
fail	fāl
fall	fôl
model	**mŏd′** l
refer	rĭ **fûr′**
education	ĕj′ ə **kā′** shən
camel	**kăm′** əl

Study the complete list of sounds and symbols on page 122.

Study each pronunciation. Write the word that matches the pronunciation.

1. brāk   brick   break   broke   _____

2. kōo′ pŏn   keep   carpet   coupon   _____

3. kăn′ səl   canker   social   cancel   _____

4. āt   eight   at   ash   _____

5. spĕsh′ əl   spoil   splash   special   _____

6. brĕth   breath   broth   bright   _____

7. kôf   kiss   could   cough   _____

8. härt   heart   art   hard   _____

9. frĕsh   friend   fresh   frown   _____

10. yēld   yell   yield   yellow   _____

11. sī′ əns   science   sense   silent   _____

12. ô′ fĭs   awful   office   official   _____

13. pī′ ə **nîr′**   pioneer   painter   banner   _____

14. jûr′ nē   jury   journey   ghostly   _____

15. mā′ jər   mayor   major   margin   _____

Score: 15

Ⓓ Proofread and Write

Alec wants to do better on his history tests. He made this list of steps he plans to take. He made four spelling mistakes. Cross out the misspelled words. Write the words correctly above them.

○ 1. Buy a good paperback dictionary.

2. Reffer to old tests. Write down the questions the teacher asks in class to challenge us.

3. Use the sample answers in the book as a model.

○ 4. Make flash cards. Write a word on one side and defien it on the other side. Then practis writing each word and its meaning.

5. Ask for an exampel of ideas that I do not understand.

○

Writing Portfolio

Think of a goal that you have in school or at your job. List some steps you could take to reach that goal. Use at least four list words.

Proofread your list carefully and correct any mistakes. Then make a clean copy and put it in your writing portfolio.

22 Learning from Mistakes

Ⓐ Check the Meaning

Read the paragraph below. Think about the meaning of the words in bold type.

How you deal with mistakes can **reveal** a lot about you. Do you spend lots of **energy** claiming that some mistake is not your **fault**? Do you want everyone's **approval**? Have a high **opinion** of yourself, but know that you aren't perfect. Face your mistakes and try to do better. Don't blame them on someone else. It's true that mistakes can **produce** bad feelings. But a mistake can be a tool for **growth** when you let it **guide** future actions. Try to figure out what really went wrong. For example, were you late to work because the bus was late? Do you **believe** that is the **probable** reason? Perhaps you got up too late. If you are not honest with yourself, you cannot improve.

Write each word in bold type next to its meaning. Check your answers in the Mini-Dictionary.

_____ **1.** the strength to do things; effort

_____ **2.** to accept as being true

_____ **3.** to create or cause

_____ **4.** the process of aging or developing

_____ **5.** to make known or to show to others

_____ **6.** likely to happen

_____ **7.** a good or favorable judgment

_____ **8.** a belief about something or someone

_____ **9.** a weakness or shortcoming

_____ **10.** to lead or direct

Score: ⟋ 10

B Study the Spelling

Word List

guide	fault	energy	believe	probable
opinion	produce	approval	reveal	growth

Form a list word by adding letters from the first column to letters in the second column. Write the list word.

be	veal	1._____
en	ion	2._____
prob	al	3._____
opin	lieve	4._____
approv	able	5._____
re	ergy	6._____

Write the list word or words for each clue.

7. There is an *ie* in its spelling. _____

8. This word is formed from the word *grow*. _____

9. It has six letters and three syllables. _____

10. They have five letters and one syllable.

_____   _____

11. There is a double consonant in its spelling. _____

12. The word *pin* is part of its spelling. _____

13. It rhymes with *vault*. _____

14. It begins like *guess* and ends like *slide*. _____

One word in each group is misspelled. Circle the misspelled word. Write it correctly.

15. energy	fualt	growth	_____
16. gide	approval	reveal	_____
17. probable	opinion	praduce	_____
18. growth	beleive	energy	_____

Score: ___/18

ⓒ Build Your Skills

Language Tutor

Use a comma between the day of the month and the year. Use a comma between a city and state.

November 4, 1996   Chicago, Illinois

When a date or address comes in the middle of a sentence, use a comma after it as well.

On November 4, 1996, Carlos bought a car.
He drove to Chicago, Illinois, and back.

Write the dates and addresses correctly.

1. August 23 1995

_____

2. Tempe Arizona

_____

3. Detroit Michigan

_____

4. Miami Florida

_____

5. July 17 1971

_____

6. Albany New York

_____

7. October 10 1969

_____

8. Austin Texas

_____

9. February 14 1994

_____

10. Juneau Alaska

_____

Write these sentences. Add commas where they are needed.

11. On November 7 1995 elections were held in every state.

_____

12. One candidate visited Miami Florida.

_____

13. A rally is planned on October 10 1998 in the Super Dome.

_____

14. The bus stopped in Stowe Vermont and Erie Pennsylvania.

_____

15. Both candidates stopped in Nashua New Hampshire during the campaign.

_____

Score: ____ / 15

Ⓓ Proofread and Write

Janice recorded some of her thoughts in a journal. This page from her journal has three spelling mistakes. Janice also forgot one comma. Cross out the misspelled words. Write the words correctly above them. Add the comma where it belongs.

On Friday, August 23 1996, I went to the new department store and tried to get a job there. I beleive I would be good at sales. I listen well and usually earn the aproval of co-workers. I got an application, but I could not fill it out. I needed the dates of my other jobs, and I could not remember them. I also needed to produce some form of identification, but I did not have any with me. I took the forms home and will fill them out there. Next time, I will know what I need. However, I do have a high opinion of the store. Everyone seemed very nice and full of enerjy. I think I would enjoy working there.

Writing Portfolio

Write a journal entry on another piece of paper. Tell about an event that taught you something. Use at least four list words.

Proofread your journal entry carefully and correct any mistakes. Then make a clean copy and put it in your writing portfolio.

Using Time Well

Ⓐ Check the Meaning

Read the paragraph below. Think about the meaning of the words in bold type.

Like money, time is a **resource** that you can use well or poorly. You will get more done if you learn to **manage** time well. One step is to make lists of what you need to do. First write all the events in **random** order, but later **arrange** them in order of importance. Not every event has **equal** importance. A job interview can have a **serious** effect on your life; a shopping trip will not. Once you have decided which events **qualify** as important ones, **label** them in some way. Then **focus** on those first. If you **combine** your list with a good calendar, you will remember all the important events. You can then see how much time you have to enjoy the other events on your list.

Write each word in bold type next to its meaning. Check your answers in the Mini-Dictionary.

_____ **1.** to place in a special way

_____ **2.** to make the center of attention

_____ **3.** to join or put together

_____ **4.** having no special order

_____ **5.** to mark or identify something

_____ **6.** to direct or control

_____ **7.** to meet certain requirements

_____ **8.** a supply of a useful element

_____ **9.** important; not silly

_____ **10.** in the same amount

Score: ⁄ 10

B Study the Spelling

Word List

focus	random	equal	resource	arrange
qualify	serious	label	combine	manage

Write the list word or words for each clue.

1. It has a double consonant in its spelling. _____

2. It begins with the prefix *com-*. _____

3. It contains the word *source*. _____

4. It ends with *age*. _____

5. It has two syllables. The first syllable has just one letter. _____

6. They have three syllables. The second syllable is *i*.

_____   _____

Write the word that does not belong in the group.

7. equal   serious   furious   _____

8. qualify   random   dignify   _____

9. combine   compact   arrange   _____

10. resource   remark   serious   _____

Add the missing letters. Write the list word.

11. lab___ ___

_____

12. seri___ ___ ___

_____

13. reso___r___e

_____

14. fo___ ___s

_____

15. rand___ ___

_____

16. qual___f___

_____

Write the list word you see in each of these words.

17. rearrange _____

18. disqualify _____

19. mismanage _____

20. equality _____

Score: ___/20

Ⓒ Build Your Skills

Language Tutor

Use commas to separate three or more items in a series.

The cook will combine <u>water</u>, <u>flour</u>, and <u>salt</u>.
                 1   **2**   **3**

<u>Write</u>, <u>proofread</u>, and <u>correct</u> your papers by Monday.
  1   **2**   **3**

Write these sentences. Draw a line under the three items. Then add commas where they are needed.

1. Be sure to bring your notebook pencil and paper.

_____

2. Are you a doctor a dentist or a nurse?

_____

3. I love to jump in the pool swim to the other side and float on my back.

_____

4. The storm struck every city town and village in the state.

_____

5. I can work late on Monday Tuesday or Friday.

_____

6. The sport requires skating blocking and passing.

_____

7. Dr. Chu Mr. Westover and Ms. Gomez will arrange the meeting.

_____

8. The study will focus on Los Angeles New York and Chicago.

_____

9. I must work on Memorial Day Halloween and Christmas this year.

_____

10. We must decide on a time a place and a day for the rally.

_____

11. Rowena always carries a calendar a notebook and a pen.

_____

12. Identify your first second and third most important events.

_____

Ⓓ Proofread and Write

Aaron keeps a list of things he needs to do. He checks them off when they are done. His list has three spelling mistakes. Aaron also forgot two commas. Cross out the misspelled words. Write the words correctly above them. Then add the commas.

Things To Do

✓ Arange for someone to take care of the cat this weekend.

✓ Buy small, medium and large envelopes.

Order new labels.

See if I can combien my two bank accounts into one.

✓ Pick up milk bread, and cheese for tonight.

✓ Find out if I quallify for low-cost loans.

Find out if Frank is serious about letting me use his computer.

Get Don to manage my grass cutting business while I am gone.

Writing Portfolio

Make a list of things you need to do. Use your own paper. Use at least four list words.

Proofread your list carefully and correct any mistakes. Make a clean copy and put it in your writing portfolio.

New Ideas

Ⓐ Check the Meaning

Read the paragraph below. Think about the meaning of the words in bold type.

Where and how do people get new ideas? Everyone has some **degree** of talent at this. However, some kinds of **behavior** are more likely to lead to new ideas. One way to develop new ideas is to **brainstorm** with other people. Choose a problem and have everyone suggest ideas. At first, do not **disagree** with any idea or **measure** its worth. A poor idea can lead to a better one. Later, judge the ideas. Some you will throw out. But you might **reflect** on others and **conclude** that they have good points. You can then **revise** them to make them better. Another way to get ideas is to become **curious** about what would happen under new conditions. Ask, "What if . . . ?" and then **imagine** all the things that might result.

Write each word in bold type next to its meaning. Check your answers in the Mini-Dictionary.

_____ **1.** to consider a problem by sharing ideas with others

_____ **2.** to find out the size or worth of something

_____ **3.** a way of acting

_____ **4.** to change in order to make better

_____ **5.** an amount of something

_____ **6.** to picture or see in your mind

_____ **7.** to think back upon

_____ **8.** wanting to know or learn more

_____ **9.** to have a different opinion

_____ **10.** to think over and decide

B Study the Spelling

Word List

brainstorm	measure	conclude	reflect	behavior
disagree	curious	revise	degree	imagine

Each word below is formed from a list word. Write the list word.

1. disagreeable _____ 4. reflection _____

2. conclusion _____ 5. imagination _____

3. curiousness _____ 6. measurable _____

Write the list words with two syllables. Draw a line between the syllables.

7. _____ 10. _____

8. _____ 11. _____

9. _____ 12. _____

Write the list word or words for each clue.

13. It is made from two words. _____

14. They begin with the *re-* prefix.

_____ _____

15. It is formed from the word *behave*. _____

16. It rhymes with *furious*. _____

17. The word *sure* is part of its spelling. _____

18. They end with a double vowel.

_____ _____

Add the missing syllable. Write the list word.

19. _____agree _____ 21. i_____ine _____

20. curi_____ _____ 22. be_____ior _____

Score: ___/22

C Build Your Skills

Language Tutor

A business letter has eight main parts: a return address, the date, an inside address, a greeting, a body, a closing, a signature, and the writer's identification. Study the example on the next page.

The envelope also has a special form. The envelope below goes with the letter on the next page.

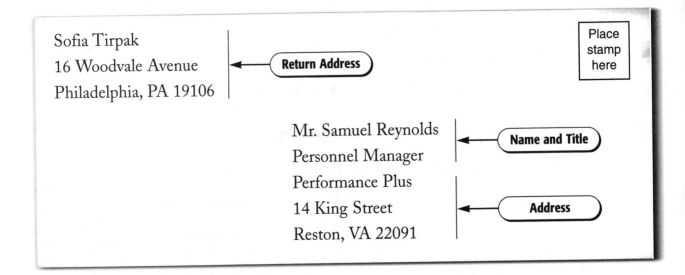

Sofia Tirpak
16 Woodvale Avenue
Philadelphia, PA 19106

Return Address

Place stamp here

Mr. Samuel Reynolds
Personnel Manager
Performance Plus
14 King Street
Reston, VA 22091

Name and Title

Address

Study the envelope and the letter on the next page. Answer each question below.

1. Who sent this letter? _____

2. To whom is the letter being sent? _____

3. What is Mr. Reynolds' title? _____

4. What company does Mr. Reynolds work for? _____

5. What kind of punctuation follows the greeting in the letter?

_____

6. What kind of punctuation follows the closing in the letter?

_____

7. Where are commas used in the address? _____

8. Does a comma come before the ZIP code? _____

Score: / 8

Ⓓ Proofread and Write

Sofia Tirpak wrote this letter to Samuel Reynolds. She made four spelling mistakes. Cross out the misspelled words. Write the words correctly above them.

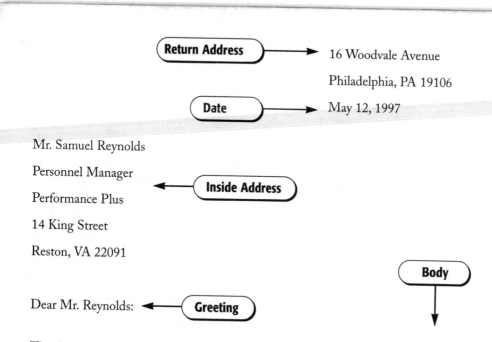

Return Address → 16 Woodvale Avenue
Philadelphia, PA 19106

Date → May 12, 1997

Mr. Samuel Reynolds
Personnel Manager
Performance Plus ← Inside Address
14 King Street
Reston, VA 22091

Body

Dear Mr. Reynolds: ← Greeting

Thank you for taking the time to talk to our group. I am always cureous about new ways to solve problems. You gave us a lot to reflect on. From now on, we will brainstom to solve problems on the production line. We will no doubt revise how we do a number of things.

Some people are afraid to dissagree. You clearly showed us how that behavior limited fresh ideas. You made us feel like a team, and I imajine that you were recommended for that reason. Thank you for an interesting and useful workshop. I will let you know about our group's progress.

Sincerely, ← Closing

Signature → *Sofia Tirpak*

Sofia Tirpak ← Writer's Identification

Writing Portfolio

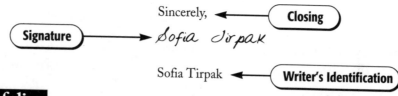

Write a business letter of your own on another piece of paper. You might thank a business owner for good service or ask for information. Use at least four list words.

Proofread your letter carefully and correct any mistakes. Then make a clean copy to mail to the business or put in your writing portfolio.

Unit 6 Review

Finish the Meaning

Fill in the circle next to the word that best completes each sentence.

1. I have always admired Martin Luther King, Jr. He is a(n) _____ we can all follow.

   Ⓐ community   Ⓒ agency
   Ⓑ model   Ⓓ resource

2. I am not sure how much carpet to order. We need to _____ the room.

   Ⓐ fail   Ⓒ include
   Ⓑ complete   Ⓓ measure

3. What does this word mean? We must check a _____.

   Ⓐ dictionary   Ⓒ modem
   Ⓑ booklet   Ⓓ merchant

4. I must get myself in good shape. Running a long race is quite a (an) _____.

   Ⓐ example   Ⓒ opportunity
   Ⓑ challenge   Ⓓ career

5. No one knew when Ed might be called. Names were read in _____ order.

   Ⓐ random   Ⓒ religious
   Ⓑ serious   Ⓓ natural

6. It was the usher's job to _____ the no-smoking rule at the movie theater.

   Ⓐ debate   Ⓒ enforce
   Ⓑ determine   Ⓓ deceive

7. The doctor was not sure about the problem. She decided to _____ me to someone else.

   Ⓐ recycle   Ⓒ recognize
   Ⓑ reflect   Ⓓ refer

8. No one can enter the work area without the _____ of the crew leader.

   Ⓐ opinion   Ⓒ qualities
   Ⓑ approval   Ⓓ system

9. I wanted to learn about our town history. The library was a great _____ for information.

   Ⓐ resource   Ⓒ committee
   Ⓑ example   Ⓓ requirement

10. We should fix the problem now. If we wait, it will get more _____.

    Ⓐ official   Ⓒ special
    Ⓑ serious   Ⓓ exact

11. The marchers hoped to _____ attention on the problem of poverty.

    Ⓐ focus   Ⓒ assemble
    Ⓑ conclude   Ⓓ dispute

12. Bad brakes were the _____ cause of the accident.

    Ⓐ legal   Ⓒ historic
    Ⓑ equal   Ⓓ probable

GO ON ➡

Check the Spelling

Fill in the circle next to the word that is spelled correctly and best completes each sentence.

13. In the United States, we _____ all people have certain rights.

  Ⓐ beleive   Ⓒ believe
  Ⓑ balieve   Ⓓ beleve

14. I found mistakes in my paper, so I had to _____ it.

  Ⓐ revise   Ⓒ ravise
  Ⓑ revice   Ⓓ revize

15. A good football player must _____ speed and strength.

  Ⓐ combin   Ⓒ combine
  Ⓑ combien   Ⓓ cumbine

16. To get ahead, you need a good _____.

  Ⓐ education   Ⓒ educasion
  Ⓑ ejucation   Ⓓ educatun

17. The teacher does not allow bad _____ in class.

  Ⓐ behaveur   Ⓒ behavor
  Ⓑ bahavior   Ⓓ behavior

18. I cannot _____ how the snake escaped.

  Ⓐ imagin   Ⓒ imagine
  Ⓑ imagune   Ⓓ imagen

19. The judge decided the damage was not my _____.

  Ⓐ fault   Ⓒ fualt
  Ⓑ falt   Ⓓ falte

20. The victim of the crime was allowed to make a _____.

  Ⓐ statment   Ⓒ statemant
  Ⓑ statement   Ⓓ staitment

21. Jack and I decided to _____ until we solved the problem.

  Ⓐ brainstorm   Ⓒ brainstorme
  Ⓑ branestorm   Ⓓ branstorm

22. Our long hours of work began to _____ results.

  Ⓐ praduce   Ⓒ produse
  Ⓑ prodoce   Ⓓ produce

23. It took hours of _____ to learn my new job.

  Ⓐ praktice   Ⓒ practice
  Ⓑ practize   Ⓓ practus

24. We need someone to _____ us through the museum.

  Ⓐ guide   Ⓒ quide
  Ⓑ giude   Ⓓ guied

STOP

Score: _____ / 24

Post-test

Part 1 Meaning

For each item below, fill in the letter next to the word or phrase that most nearly expresses the meaning of the first word.

Sample

1. hammer
- (A) part of the arm
- ● a tool used for driving nails
- (C) a type of vegetable
- (D) to mix thoroughly

---

1. convention
- (A) a strong belief
- (B) an important event
- (C) a meeting
- (D) a type of entertainment

2. combine
- (A) to explode with great force
- (B) to comfort
- (C) to bring together
- (D) to search thoroughly

3. curious
- (A) requiring many people
- (B) unkind
- (C) have a desire to know
- (D) not legal

4. resource
- (A) to provide with additional supplies
- (B) a source of help
- (C) one who lives in a particular place
- (D) a sticky material

5. focus
- (A) the center of great interest
- (B) simple
- (C) old beliefs or customs
- (D) a loyal follower

6. opinion
- (A) an entrance or exit
- (B) a belief
- (C) one who works against an idea
- (D) a dull surface

7. evidence
- (A) an evil plan
- (B) facts that lead to a belief
- (C) someone with limited abilities
- (D) someone who hides from the law

8. debate
- (A) to move away from
- (B) to compare
- (C) to mislead or confuse
- (D) to argue for or against something

9. qualify
- (A) to announce
- (B) to satisfy certain requirements
- (C) to rule against
- (D) to put out a fire

10. patriot
- (A) someone who loves and defends his or her country
- (B) a tropical bird
- (C) someone who is being treated by a doctor
- (D) a large, open building

GO ON ➡

Part 2 Spelling

For each item below, fill in the letter next to the correct spelling of the word.

11. Ⓐ excellant Ⓒ excellent
    Ⓑ excellunt Ⓓ excelent

12. Ⓐ Saturday Ⓒ Saterday
    Ⓑ Satirday Ⓓ Sadurday

13. Ⓐ representative Ⓒ reprasentative
    Ⓑ representive Ⓓ representitive

14. Ⓐ resourse Ⓒ resurse
    Ⓑ resoeurse Ⓓ resource

15. Ⓐ dispuet Ⓒ disput
    Ⓑ dispute Ⓓ despute

16. Ⓐ revalution Ⓒ revolution
    Ⓑ revolushun Ⓓ revolusion

17. Ⓐ machinery Ⓒ machinary
    Ⓑ mashinery Ⓓ machenry

18. Ⓐ develope Ⓒ davelop
    Ⓑ develop Ⓓ develup

19. Ⓐ conscent Ⓒ consant
    Ⓑ concent Ⓓ consent

20. Ⓐ poisen Ⓒ poison
    Ⓑ pioson Ⓓ poisun

21. Ⓐ swallow Ⓒ swalow
    Ⓑ swallowe Ⓓ swallou

22. Ⓐ opportunaty Ⓒ oppurtunity
    Ⓑ opportunity Ⓓ oportunity

23. Ⓐ advancement Ⓒ advancment
    Ⓑ advansement Ⓓ addvancment

24. Ⓐ retirment Ⓒ retirmant
    Ⓑ retirement Ⓓ retierment

25. Ⓐ earnst Ⓒ earnest
    Ⓑ ernest Ⓓ earnist

26. Ⓐ conclud Ⓒ cunclude
    Ⓑ conklude Ⓓ conclude

27. Ⓐ serious Ⓒ serios
    Ⓑ serius Ⓓ scerious

28. Ⓐ treety Ⓒ tready
    Ⓑ treaty Ⓓ treidy

29. Ⓐ demacratic Ⓒ demecratic
    Ⓑ democratic Ⓓ demmocratic

30. Ⓐ religous Ⓒ religius
    Ⓑ raligious Ⓓ religious

STOP

Score: ☐ / 30

How to Use the Dictionary

Letters and symbols give the **pronunciation**. Use the pronunciation key to sound out the word.

The **part of speech** is given after the pronunciation.

The **definition** tells you the meaning. When there is more than one meaning, each meaning is numbered.

Each **word** is listed in alphabetical order and separated into syllables.

Two different **words with the same spelling** are numbered.

Sometimes a **sample sentence** is given to make the definition clearer.

Sometimes you will be told to look up a **simpler form** of the word.

Other forms of the word are often shown.

o·pen /ō′ pən/ —*adj.* **1.** Not closed; allowing passage in and out: *The cow got out of the pen through the open gate.* **2.** Available for business: *The store is open most evenings.* —*verb* To uncover or unwrap; to unfasten.

pen[1] /pĕn/ —*noun* A tool for writing.

pen[2] a fenced-in area, often used to keep animals.

ran /răn/ —*verb* The past form of *run*: *We ran to the bus stop.*

run /rŭn/ —*verb* **ran, running 1.** To move quickly on foot: *Horses run faster than people.* **2.** To move around freely: *Don't let your pets run through the neighborhood.*

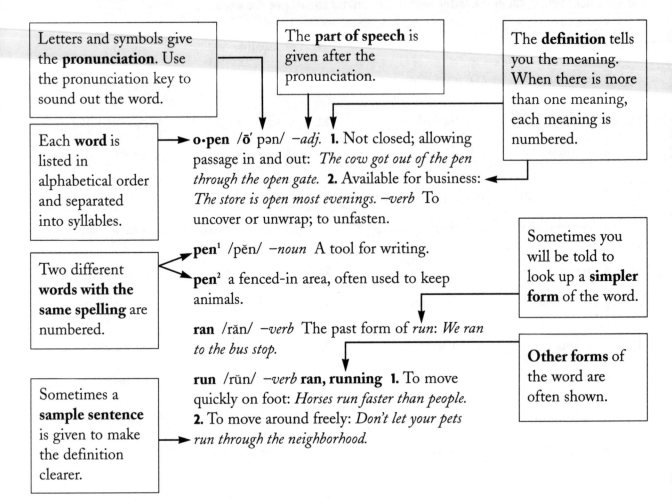

Pronunciation Key

ă	cat	ī	ice	o͞o	food	hw	which
ā	day	î	near	yo͞o	cute	zh	usual
â	care	ŏ	hot	o͝o	book	ə	about
ä	father	ō	go	ŭ	drum		open
ĕ	wet	ô	law	û	fur		pencil
ē	see	oi	oil	th	this		lemon
ĭ	pit	ou	out	th	thin		circus

Mini-Dictionary

ab·sorb /əb **sôrb**'/ *-verb* To soak up: *Use a rag to absorb the spilled oil.*

ac·ci·dent /**ăk**' sĭ dənt/ *-noun* An unplanned happening, often a mistake: *Pay attention when you drive or you will cause an accident.*

ac·cuse /ə **kyōōz**'/ *-verb* To charge, or blame, someone with doing something wrong.

ache /āk/ *-noun* A dull pain: *I must see a doctor about this ache.* *-verb* **ached, aching, aches.** To feel a dull pain: *Tim's legs ached after the road race.*

ad·just /ə **jŭst**'/ *-verb* To change to meet certain conditions, adapt: *The workers had to adjust their habits because of the new machines.*

ad·vance·ment /ăd **văns**' mənt/ *-noun* **1.** State of going forward or getting better. **2.** Promotion: *People who work hard are rewarded with career advancement.*

ad·vice /ăd **vīs**'/ *-noun* Suggestion about how to solve a problem or achieve a goal: *Greg asked for advice on how to fix the leak.*

ad·vo·cate /**ăd**' və kāt'/ *-verb* To argue in favor of; support; urge. /**ăd**' və kĭt/ *-noun* Person who argues in favor of.

a·gen·cy /**ā**' jən sē/ *-noun* A business or company that helps achieve a goal: *I will contact a real estate agency to help me sell my house.*

an·nu·al /**ăn**' yōō əl/ *-adj.* **1.** Happening once a year. **2.** Measured by one year's time: *The annual rainfall was higher this year than last year.*

a·part·ment /ə **pärt**' mənt/ *-noun* A room or group of rooms to live in, usually part of a building where other people live in separate units: *Her apartment had a sunny kitchen and a balcony.*

ap·pli·ca·tion /**ăp** lĭ **kā**' shən/ *-noun* A form used for making a request: *Mary filled out an application for a library card so that she could borrow books.*

ap·point·ment /ə **point**' mənt/ *-noun* Agreement to meet at a specific time and place: *Greg has an appointment at the employment office at ten o'clock on Tuesday.*

ap·prov·al /ə **prōō**' vəl/ *-noun* **1.** Favorable judgment: *He gained his supervisor's approval through hard work.* **2.** Permission.

ar·range /ə **rānj**'/ *-verb* **1.** To put in order. **2.** To plan for.

ar·rest /ə **rĕst**'/ *-verb* To hold or capture under authority of law or for breaking a law.

as·sem·ble /ə **sĕm**' bəl/ *-verb* To gather together into a group: *Assemble the tools you will need before you begin.*

ath·lete /**ăth**' lēt'/ *-noun* A person who trains for and participates in sports: *Tina is quite an athlete: she swims, runs, and plays tennis.*

at·tempt /ə **tĕmpt**'/ *-verb* To try, make an effort: *I will attempt to convince him, but I cannot make any promises.*

av·er·age /**ăv**' ər ĭj/ or /**ăv**' rĭj/ *-adj.* **1.** Common, ordinary, usual: *The average car runs for five to ten years.* **2.** The number found by dividing the sum of a set of quantities by the number of quantities in the set.

a·ware /ə **wâr**'/ *-adj.* Knowing, realizing, recognizing: *Are you aware of tomorrow's meeting?*

bank /băngk/ *-noun* An organization for saving, investing, borrowing, or exchanging money: *Sue keeps her money in the bank, where it is safe and earns interest.*

be·ha·vior /bĭ **hāv**′ yər/ -*noun* The way one acts in certain situations: *People will look at your behavior to see if you are a good worker.*

be·lieve /bĭ **lēv**′/ -*verb* To accept as true: *I believe your story because I know you always tell the truth.*

ben·e·fit /**bĕn**′ ə fĭt/ -*noun* **1.** Payment made in cash, services, or time as part of an agreement: *The benefit package for this job includes health insurance, vacation time, and child care.* **2.** Something helpful.

bill·board /**bĭl**′ bôrd′/ -*noun* A large sign used for advertising, usually outdoors: *I saw the hotel advertised on a billboard by the highway.*

book·let /**boŏk**′ lĭt/ -*noun* A small book: *We received a booklet on employee benefits.*

bot·tle /**bŏt**′ l/ -*noun* Storage container with a narrow neck that can be capped or stopped, especially one for liquids.

brain·storm /**brān**′ stôrm′/ -*verb* To consider a problem, to work to find an idea or solution.

break /brāk/ -*verb* **broke, broken, breaking. 1.** To separate into pieces, come apart. **2.** To become unusable, stop working: *If the machine breaks, we will not be able to finish this order.*

breath /brĕth/ -*noun* The air taken into and expelled from the lungs: *On cold days you can see your breath.*

bro·ken /**brō**′ kən/ -*adj.* Past participle of *break.* Split into pieces, damaged, or not working.

build·ing /**bĭl**′ dĭng/ -*noun* A large structure made of long-lasting materials and intended to remain in place: *The new building will make a great teen center when it is done.*

cab·i·net /**kăb**′ ə nĭt/ -*noun* **1.** Group of advisors chosen by the head of a country. **2.** A cupboardlike case for storing and displaying items.

ca·reer /kə **rîr**′/ -*noun* **1.** A line of work: *José is studying for a career in computer science.* **2.** The path of one's working life.

cause /kôz/ -*verb* **caused, causing, causes.** To make happen, bring about: *Speed will cause accidents.*

cel·e·brate /**sĕl**′ ə brāt′/ -*verb* **celebrated, celebrating, celebrates.** To mark with special activities: *We always celebrate my birthday at Grandma's house.*

chal·lenge /**chăl**′ ənj/ -*noun* A task or goal that requires great energy or ability: *Driving in the rain can be quite a challenge.*

charge /chärj/ -*noun* **1.** The amount of money asked for as payment: *The charge for our dinner was $36.* **2.** Responsibility.

chill /chĭl/ -*verb* To cool, to reduce the temperature of: *Be sure to chill the pudding before you serve it.*

Christ·mas /**krĭs**′ məs/ -*noun* The day Christians celebrate the birth of Jesus, December 25.

church /chûrch/ -*noun* A place where people meet to worship or pray: *We will attend Christmas services at the church.*

cit·i·zen /**sĭt**′ ĭ zən/ -*noun* A member of a country, either by birth or by choice, who has certain rights and responsibilities.

com·bine /kəm **bīn**′/ -*verb* To bring together, unite.

com·mit·tee /kə **mĭt**′ ē/ -*noun* A group of people chosen to do a job or make a recommendation.

com·mu·ni·ty /kə **myōō**′ nĭ tē/ -*noun* A group of people who live together or share a common interest: *The school community includes parents as well as students and teachers.*

com·pa·ny /kŭm′ pə nē/ –*noun* **1.** A business organization: *Todd worked for the same company all his life.* **2.** A group of people organized for a specific purpose, such as an acting company or military unit. **3.** Guest or guests.

com·pare /kəm pâr′/ –*verb* To consider how things are alike and different: *Always compare prices at different stores when buying a costly item.*

com·plain /kəm plān′/ –*verb* To point out faults or problems: *If you do not get the service you want, complain to the manager.*

com·plete /kəm plēt′/ –*adj.* Having no parts missing: *A complete medical history has family information as well as information about the patient.*

com·pli·ance /kəm plī′ əns/ –*noun* The act of behaving in agreement with a request, command, or law.

com·ply /kəm plī′/ –*verb* To do what is required by a law or rule, or to agree to a request: *The boss will comply with Sam's request for extra sick time.*

com·pu·ter /kəm pyoo′ tər/ –*noun* A machine that stores and processes information: *My doctor keeps all his patients' records on the computer.*

con·clude /kən klood′/ –*verb* **1.** To consider and decide. **2.** To bring to an end.

con·di·tion /kən dĭsh′ ən/ –*noun* State of fitness, readiness for use: *The house is in poor condition; no one could live in it.*

Con·gress /kŏng′ grĭs/ –*noun* The branch of the U.S. government that makes laws.

con·sent /kən sĕnt′/ –*noun* Approval, permission: *I need the boss's consent to take a day off next week.*

con·se·quence /kŏn′ sĭ kwĕns′/ –*noun* The result, outcome: *Good health is a consequence of good habits.*

con·sti·tu·tion /kŏn′ stĭ too′ shən/ or /kŏn′ stĭ tyoo′ shən/ –*noun* **1.** The basic principles governing a nation, state, or other formally organized group. **2.** The document stating these principles.

con·sult /kən sŭlt′/ –*verb* To ask for advice or information from: *Before beginning an exercise program, always consult your doctor.*

con·tin·ue /kən tĭn′ yoo/ –*verb* To keep on happening as before: *We will continue studying this lesson.*

con·tract /kŏn′ trăkt′/ –*noun* An agreement, usually one in writing: *This year's contract includes a 5 percent raise for all employees.*

con·ven·tion /kən vĕn′ shən/ –*noun* A meeting or gathering, usually of a large group: *Tom attended the state teachers' convention last week.*

con·vict /kən vĭkt′/ –*verb* To prove and declare someone guilty of a crime. /kŏn′ vĭkt/ –*noun* Person serving a prison term.

cough /kôf/ –*noun* A condition in which air is forced out of the lungs and produces a noise: *Sal suffered from a cold, cough, and fever.* –*verb* To force air out of the lungs.

cou·pon /koo′ pŏn′ or kyoo′ pŏn′/ –*noun* Ticket allowing the holder to receive something, often a discount on a purchase: *You can save a lot of money by using coupons from the newspaper.*

court /kôrt/ –*noun* **1.** A place where legal decisions are made. **2.** A place marked off for a game such as tennis, basketball, or volleyball.

credit /krĕd′ ĭt/ –*noun* Reputation for honoring a debt: *Fred has good credit because he always pays his bills on time.*

cu·ri·ous /kyoor′ ē əs/ –*adj.* Wanting to know or learn more.

dam·age /dăm′ ĭj/ -*verb* To harm, hurt, or injure something and thereby reduce its value or usefulness: *The rocks and sticks damaged the lawn mower.*

dan·ger·ous /dān′ jər əs/ -*adj.* Unsafe, could be harmful: *Driving when you are sleepy can be very dangerous.*

de·bate /dĭ băt′/ -*verb* **1.** To consider arguments for and against a question or issue. **2.** To argue in public following set rules. -*noun* A formal argument.

de·cay /dĭ kā′/ -*noun* The act or result of the process of rotting or declining: *The old, crumbling building was full of decay.*

de·ceive /dĭ sēv′/ -*verb* To trick, mislead, or cheat someone: *The ad deceived us by making us think the item was larger than it really is.*

de·ci·sion /dĭ sĭzh′ ən/ -*noun* A conclusion, determination: *We will make a decision about the hike after we hear the weather report.*

ded·i·cate /dĕd′ ĭ kāt′/ -*verb* To set aside for a specific use: *We will dedicate next week to spring cleaning.*

de·fense /dĭ fĕns′/ -*noun* The act of protecting from attack, danger, or harm.

de·fine /dĭ fīn′/ -*verb* **1.** To make clear or distinct: *If you define your goals for the meeting, you will get more done.* **2.** To state the exact meaning of a word or idea.

de·gree /dĭ grē′/ -*noun* A unit of measurement; an amount.

dem·o·crat·ic /dĕm′ ə krăt′ ĭk/ -*adj.* Government by the people.

den·tist /dĕn′ tĭst/ -*noun* Person trained and licensed to care for the teeth and mouth: *Mark needed a dentist to fix the tooth he broke when he fell.*

de·part·ment /dĭ pärt′ mənt/ -*noun* A part of a business or other organization with specific duties or responsibilities: *Take your bill to the accounting department.*

de·pos·it /dĭ pŏz′ ĭt/ -*verb* To put or lay down; to put in a bank: *If you deposit your money in the bank, you will always know where it is.*

de·ter·mine /dĭ tûr′ mĭn/ -*verb* To make a firm decision: *We will determine the best plan after careful study.*

de·vel·op /dĭ vĕl′ əp/ -*verb* To bring about in stages: *We need a plan to develop a new product.*

dic·tion·ar·y /dĭk′ shə nĕr′ ē/ -*noun* A book listing words in alphabetical order and giving their meaning, pronunciation, and other information about them.

dif·fi·cult /dĭf′ ĭ kŭlt′/ -*adj.* Hard to do, not easy: *It is sometimes difficult to learn a new job, but the rewards are usually worth it.*

dis·a·gree /dĭs′ ə grē′/ -*verb* To have a different opinion; to see or understand something differently.

dis·cuss /dĭ skŭs′/ -*verb* To talk over in an open manner, considering all sides of a question or issue.

di·spute /dĭ spyōōt′/ -*verb* To question or deny the truth or accuracy of something.

doc·tor /dŏk′ tər/ -*noun* Person trained and licensed to treat sick or injured people: *The doctor put a cast on Mary's broken leg.*

doc·u·ment /dŏk′ yə mənt/ -*noun* A paper with official or important information: *Your driver's license is an important document.* -*verb* To create written evidence of something.

du·ties plural of **duty**: /dōō′ tēz/ or /dyōō′ tēz/ *Sam's duties were sweeping the floor and emptying the trash.*

du·ty /dŏŏ′ tē/ or /dyŏŏ′ tē/ *-noun* Something one must or should do, a responsibility.

ear·nest /ûr′ nĭst/ *-adj.* Sincere, enthusiastic, true: *The boss recognized Carl's earnest desire to improve on the job.*

ed·u·ca·tion /ĕj′ ə kā′ shən/ *-noun* Knowledge or skill that is gained through study or experience: *An education in business will help you manage your money.*

e·lec·tric /ĭ lĕk′ trĭk/ *-adj.* Powered by electricity: *Someday we may drive electric cars.*

e·mer·gen·cy /ĭ mûr′ jən sē/ *-noun* Situation to which one must respond right away: *Prepare for an emergency by knowing what to do.*

em·ploy /ĕm ploi′/ *-verb* **1.** To hire, give work to, and pay: *The store employs more people during the busy holiday season.* **2.** To use.

en·act /ĕn ăkt′/ *-verb* To make into law.

en·er·gy /ĕn′ ər jē/ *-noun* **1.** The strength for work or for strenuous activity: *It takes a great amount of energy to change directions.* **2.** A source of power, such as electricity or gas.

en·force /ĕn fôrs′/ *-verb* To make certain that rules and laws are followed.

e·nor·mous /ĭ nôr′ məs/ *-adj.* Very large in size, degree, or number: *The box is enormous; it will take four people to carry it.*

en·vi·ron·ment /ĕn vī′ rən mənt/ *-noun* Surrounding area, conditions of the area: *A student's home environment will affect his or her schoolwork.*

e·qual /ē′ kwəl/ *-adj.* Of the same amount or quality as something else.

e·stab·lish /ĭ stăb′ lĭsh/ *-verb* To bring about, institute: *The crew established a new morning routine.*

ev·i·dence /ĕv′ ĭ dəns/ *-noun* Facts or signs showing that something is or is not true; proof.

ex·act /ĭg zăkt′/ *-adj.* To be the same in every detail, an accurate measurement: *I need an exact copy of his speech to write my report.*

ex·am·i·na·tion /ĭg zăm′ ə nā′ shən/ *-noun* **1.** A close study or inspection. **2.** A test.

ex·am·ple /ĭg zăm′ pəl/ *-noun* A person or thing that shows what others in a group are like; a sample: *Sally is an example of a good student.*

ex·cel·lent /ĕk′ sə lənt/ *-adj.* Of the highest quality, outstanding: *This pie is excellent; it is the best I have ever tasted.*

ex·plain /ĭk splān′/ *-verb* To make understandable: *Will you explain this new rule to me?*

ex·treme /ĭk strēm′/ *-adj.* Very great, the most possible: *Because of the extreme cold, the roofers could not work today.*

fail /fāl/ *-verb* To not achieve a goal; to be unsuccessful: *I failed to finish the project on time.*

fault /fôlt/ *-noun* **1.** A weakness or short-coming. **2.** Responsibility for a mistake: *I forgot to blow out the candles, so the fire was my fault.*

Feb·ru·ary /fĕb′ rŏŏ ĕr′ ē/ or /fĕb′ yŏŏ er′ ē/ *-noun* The second month of the year.

fo·cus /fō′ kəs/ *-verb* To concentrate on, to attend to one thing while disregarding others.

for·bid /fôr bĭd′/ *-verb* To not allow a person or persons to do something; prohibit.

for·eign /fôr′ ĭn/ or /fŏr′ ĭn/ *-adj.* From or in a country other than one's own: *Kerry is studying foreign languages because she would like to travel to other countries.*

Friday–knowledge

Fri·day /frī′ dē/ or /frī′ dā/ -*noun* The sixth day of the week.

gal·lon /gǎl′ ən/ -*noun* A unit for measuring liquids equal to four quarts.

ga·rage /gə räzh′/ or /gə räj′/ -*noun* **1.** Place for storing a car. **2.** Business that repairs cars.

gas·o·line /gǎs′ ə lēn′ or gǎs′ ə lēn/ -*noun* Fuel that powers cars and trucks.

gov·ern·ment /gǔv′ ərn mənt/ -*noun* **1.** The system of organizing the affairs of a group of people. **2.** The people responsible for or employed to organize the affairs of a group: *The government decided to help the flood victims.*

growth /grōth/ -*noun* Increase as in size, age, ability, importance, or power; development: *The growth of the computer business may mean more jobs.*

guide /gīd/ -*verb* To direct the course of; lead: *Tom will guide you through the lab on your first visit.*

hab·i·tat /hǎb′ ĭ tǎt′/ -*noun* The area or place where a plant or animal naturally lives or grows.

Hal·low·een /hǎl′ ə wēn′/ or /hŏl′ ə wēn′/ -*noun* Holiday when children dress in costumes, October 31.

health·y /hěl′ thē/ -*adj.* **1.** In good health, not sick **2.** Likely to put or keep one in good health: *Fruits and vegetables are part of a healthy diet.*

heart /härt/ -*noun* The organ that pumps blood through the body: *An adult's heart beats about seventy-two times each minute.*

his·tor·ic /hĭ stor′ ĭk/ -*adj.* Well-known or important in history: *The first walk in space was a historic event.*

hol·i·day /hŏl′ ĭ dā/ -*noun* **1.** Day of celebration: *The fourth of July is my favorite holiday.* **2.** Vacation.

hos·pi·tal /hŏs′ pĭ tl/ -*noun* A place where sick or injured people are cared for: *Sally stayed at the hospital overnight after the car accident.*

ho·tel /hō těl′/ -*noun* Business that rents rooms for lodging: *We found a great hotel to stay in on our vacation.*

i·mag·ine /ĭ mǎj′ ĭn/ -*verb* To picture in one's mind.

im·prove /ĭm proov′/ -*verb* To make or get better: *The new machine will improve the shoes they are making.*

in·clude /ĭn klood′/ -*verb* **1.** Contain along with other things: *The class includes time for review.* **2.** Contain within itself.

in·crease /ĭn krēs′/ -*verb* To become or make larger in size or number: *The new menu should increase business at the restaurant.*

in·ter·est /ĭn′ trĭst/ or /ĭn′ tər ĭst/ -*noun* Fee charged or paid for the use of money: *Sally earned $50 in interest on her savings last year.*

in·ter·view /ĭn′ tər vyoo′/ -*verb* To talk with someone to get information: *We will interview several people interested in the job.*

i·o·dine /ī′ ə dīn′/ -*noun* A liquid used to kill germs: *Put iodine on your cut.*

ir·ri·tate /ĭr′ ĭ tāt′/ -*verb* **1.** To make angry. **2.** To make sore.

Jan·u·ar·y /jǎn′ yoo ěr ē/ -*noun* The first month of the year.

jus·tice /jǔs′ tĭs/ -*noun* Fairness, especially in the eyes of the law.

kitch·en /kĭch′ ən/ -*noun* A room where food is prepared and cooked.

knowl·edge /nŏl′ ĭj/ -*noun* Understanding, awareness: *Tom has a great knowledge of cars and how they work.*

la·bel /lā′ bəl/ -*verb* To identify or name something. -*noun* The tag that identifies something.

le·gal /lē′ gəl/ -*adj.* **1.** Relating to the law. **2.** Allowed under the law.

lib·er·ty /lĭb′ ər tē/ -*noun* Freedom, ability to speak and act as one chooses: *We have the liberty to say what we think.*

lo·cal /lō′ kəl/ -*adj.* Of or relating to a specific place: *I always buy local corn because it is fresher.*

ma·chin·er·y /mə shē′ nə rē/ -*noun* A group of machines, or machines in general: *The factory was filled with many kinds of machinery.*

man·age /măn′ ĭj/ -*verb* **1.** To direct or control. **2.** To succeed.

ma·te·ri·al /mə tîr′ ē əl/ -*noun* That which something is or can be made of: *I need more material to finish this project.*

meas·ure /mĕzh′ ər/ -*verb* To find out the size or value of something.

Me·mo·ri·al Day /mə môr′ ē əl dā/ -*noun* Day for remembering the dead, especially those who have died in war, May 30.

mer·chan·dise /mûr′ chən dīs′/ -*noun* Things for sale: *That store carries only the best merchandise.*

mer·chant /mûr′ chənt/ -*noun* Someone in the business of buying and selling goods for profit.

mile·age /mī′ lĭj/ -*noun* The number of miles traveled.

mis·er·a·ble /mĭz′ ər ə bəl/ or /mĭz′ rə bəl/ -*adj.* Very unhappy.

mod·el /mŏd′ l/ -*noun* A person or thing that serves as an example of something others can look to and copy: *You may use the finished table as a model when making your own.*

mo·dem /mō′ dĕm/ -*noun* A device that changes information from one format into another: *To send information from my telephone to your printer, we need a modem.*

Mon·day /mŭn′ dē/ or /mŭn′ dā/ -*noun* The second day of the week.

mon·ey /mŭn′ ē/ -*noun* Coins or paper bills with a fixed value that may be traded for goods and services.

nat·u·ral /năch′ ər əl/ or /năch′ rəl/ -*adj.* Found in or provided by nature; not made or changed by man.

ne·glect /nĭ glĕkt′/ -*verb* To ignore, not take care of: *If you neglect your plants, they will not grow.*

oc·ca·sion /ə kā′ zhən/ -*noun* An event or time: *Graduation is an occasion for celebrating.*

oc·ca·sion·al /ə kā′ zhə nəl/ -*adj.* Once in a while, not constant or continuous: *Even very healthy people have an occasional cough or cold.*

of·fer /ô′ fər/ or /ŏf′ ər/ -*verb* To express a willingness to do something, propose: *He offered to help me carry the groceries inside.*

of·fi·cial /ə fĭsh′ əl/ -*adj.* Recognized by an authority: *The United States does not have an official language.*

o·pin·ion /ə pĭn′ yən/ -*noun* A belief about someone or something: *In my opinion this is the best meal we have had here.*

op·por·tu·ni·ty /ŏp′ ər tōō′ nĭ tē/ plural **opportunities.** -*noun* A chance to do or receive something good or to achieve something one wants: *The program was an opportunity to learn new job skills.*

pa·tri·ot /pā′ trē ət/ -*noun* Person who is loyal to and supports his or her country: *John Adams was an American patriot.*

per·cent /pər **sĕnt**ʹ/ *-noun* Part per hundred: *Half the people, or fifty percent, wanted a new school budget.*

per·mit /**pûr**ʹ mĭt/ *-noun* The written proof of permission to do something: *You must have a permit to fish in that lake.* /pər **mĭt**ʹ/ *-verb* To allow.

poi·son /**poi**ʹ zən/ *-noun* Something that can harm or kill because of its action in the body or on the skin: *Many soaps and cleaners contain a poison that could hurt you if you are not careful.* *-verb* To harm or kill using a poison: *We poisoned the weeds to help the grass grow.*

prac·ti·cal /**prăk**ʹ tĭ kəl/ *-adj.* Useful, good for its purpose: *The new hammer was a practical addition to the tool chest.*

prac·tice /**prăk**ʹ tĭs/ *-verb* To repeat an action or skill to learn from it or to improve it: *Jill practiced playing the flute every day before the concert.*

pre·pare /prĭ **pâr**ʹ/ *-verb* To get ready: *Prepare for your job interview by making a list of questions to ask.*

pre·scrip·tion /prĭ **skrĭp**ʹ shən/ *-noun* A doctor's order for a medicine: *Dr. Harvey gave me a prescription for a cream to cure my rash.*

prob·a·ble /**prŏb**ʹ ə bəl/ *-adj.* Likely to happen or to be true; believable.

pro·duce /prə **doos**ʹ/ or /prə **dyoos**ʹ/ *-verb* To create, cause, or bring forth; yield.

pro·mo·tion /prə **mō**ʹ shən/ *-noun* Movement to a better or higher job, level, or class: *Ted's promotion made him the senior man in the shop.*

pro·per·ty /**prŏp**ʹ ər tē/ *-noun* A thing or things one owns: *If you take good care of your property, it will last longer.*

pub·lic /**pŭb**ʹ lĭk/ *-adj.* Open to or serving all the people, not private: *Anyone can get a card to borrow books from the public library.*

qual·i·fy /**kwŏl**ʹ ə fīʹ/ *-verb* **qualifies, qualified, qualifying.** **1.** To meet certain requirements. **2.** To restrict the meaning of.

qualities /**kwŏl**ʹ ĭ tēz/ plural of **quality**: *Honesty and hard work are qualities that lead to success.*

qual·i·ty /**kwŏl**ʹ ĭ tē/ *-noun* A feature, trait, characteristic, or ability: *He has the quality of fairness.*

ran·dom /**răn**ʹ dəm/ *-adj.* Having no special order.

rec·og·nize /**rĕk**ʹ əg nīz/ *-verb* To know again, to understand from previous experience: *By the time her youngest child had the measles, Mom recognized the symptoms.*

rec·om·mend /rĕk ə **mĕnd**ʹ/ *-verb* **1.** Suggest a course of action: *Most people recommend that you follow a careful savings plan.* **2.** Evaluate a person for something such as a job, school, or club.

re·cy·cle /rē **sī**ʹ kəl/ *-verb* To use again, or make available for reuse.

re·fer /rĭ **fûr**ʹ/ *-verb* To use as a source of information; consult: *Refer to your map for directions.*

re·flect /rĭ **flĕkt**ʹ/ *-verb* To think back on; to consider carefully and form an opinion on.

re·fund /rĭ **fŭnd**ʹ/ or /**rē**ʹ fŭndʹ/ *-verb* To give back, especially money: *If you are not happy with something you buy, ask the store to refund your money.*

re·gard·less /rĭ **gärd**ʹ lĭs/ *-adv.* Anyway, despite: *Joe ran the race regardless of his injuries.*

reg·u·late /**rĕg**ʹ yə lātʹ/ *-verb* To control or adjust using rules or systems.

re·lig·ious /rĭ **lĭj´** əs/ -*adj.* Related to belief in a higher being: *Christmas is a religious holiday.*

rep·re·sen·ta·tive /rĕp´ rĭ **zĕn´** tə tĭv/ -*adj.* Having traits or beliefs that show the traits or beliefs of a group: *Her talent as a runner is representative of her family's talent.* -*noun* Person who represents the interests of another person or a group of people.

re·quire·ment /rĭ **kwīr´** mənt/ -*noun* Something that is needed to do or receive something else: *Terry completed the last requirement for graduation from high school.*

res·i·dent /**rĕz´** ĭ dənt/ -*noun* A person who lives in a given place: *Are you a resident of Vermont or New Hampshire?*

re·source /**rē´** sôrs´/ or /rĭ **sôrs´**/ -*noun* Something useful, especially something in limited supply.

re·spond /rĭ **spŏnd´**/ -*verb* Answer, reply: *Please respond to the invitation promptly.*

re·tail /**rē´** tāl´/ -*noun* The sale of goods to the public in small amounts.

re·tire·ment /rĭ **tīr´** mənt/ -*noun* State of having left one's job or other position for good: *When Greg goes into retirement next year, he will spend more time with his family.*

re·veal /rĭ **vēl´**/ -*verb* To make known to others, to show especially something hidden or concealed.

re·view /rĭ **vyoo´**/ -*noun* An evaluation, a description pointing out strengths and weaknesses: *Jen's hard work paid off with a very good review and a raise.* -*verb* **1.** To study. **2.** To look at again. **3.** To evaluate.

re·vise /rĭ **vīz´**/ -*verb* To change in order to make better.

rev·o·lu·tion /rĕv´ ə **loo´** shən/ -*noun* The overthrow of a government, usually by those governed by it: *The United States came into being after a revolution against British rule.*

sal·a·ry /**săl´** ə rē/ -*noun* Money paid to an employee on a regular basis: *Kim's salary is so small she must work a second job to pay all her bills.*

Sat·ur·day /**săt´** ər dē/ or /**săt´** ər dā/ -*noun* The seventh day of the week.

sci·ence /**sī´** əns/ -*noun* Knowledge of nature and the physical world drawn from systematic study.

Sep·tem·ber /sĕp **tĕm´** bər/ -*noun* The ninth month of the year.

se·ri·ous /**sîr´** ē əs/ -*adj.* Important, having a significant result.

set·tle·ment /**sĕt´** l mənt/ -*noun* **1.** A small, new community. **2.** A group of people in a new country or area; colonization. **3.** A final or complete payment.

sig·nal /**sĭg´** nəl/ -*noun* An action, word, or thing that gives information or a warning: *Do not start the motor until I give you the signal.*

sim·i·lar /**sĭm´** ə lər/ -*adj.* The same as something else in most but not all respects: *The blouse in the discount store is similar to the one in the department store.*

sleep·y /**slē´** pē/ -*adj.* **sleepier, sleepiest.** Drowsy, tired, ready to sleep: *After an exciting day at the county fair, the children were all sleepy.*

slo·gan /**slō´** gən/ -*noun* Saying or phrase used to identify or promote something.

smoke /smōk/ -*verb* **smoked, smoking, smokes.** To inhale and exhale the smoke from a cigarette, cigar, or pipe: *You may smoke cigarettes in this restaurant, but not cigars.*

smoking–yield

smok·ing /smō′ kĭng/ –*verb* present participle of *smoke*: *Many companies offer programs to help employees quit smoking.*

spe·cial /spĕsh əl/ –*adj.* Made for a limited purpose, not like others: *Amy took a special class to update her office skills.*

state·ment /stāt′ mənt/ –*noun* A sentence that gives information, states something.

stren·u·ous /strĕn′ yōō əs/ –*adj.* Very demanding, difficult: *After a strenuous hike, they were all glad to rest at the mountain top.*

suc·cess /sək sĕs′/ –*noun* Person or thing that achieves the desired results: *The popular play was a great success.*

Sun·day /sŭn′ dē/ or /sŭn′ dā/ –*noun* The first day of the week.

su·pe·ri·or /sōō pîr′ ē ər/ –*adj.* Of the highest quality, better than all others, the best: *There are many good workers, but only a few are superior.*

swal·low /swŏl′ ō/ –*verb* To cause something to pass down one's own throat into the stomach, to drink or eat: *Children do not always chew enough before they swallow.*

sys·tem /sĭs′ təm/ –*noun* A plan or method for doing something, a routine: *Our delivery system gets the goods to the customers quickly.*

tab·let /tăb′ lĭt/ –*noun* A flat pill: *Roy took an aspirin tablet for his headache.*

tax /tăks/ –*noun* Payment people, groups, and businesses must make to the government: *The new tax will help build better roads in our town.*

teeth /tēth/ –*noun* plural of **tooth.**

tem·po·rar·y /tĕm′ pə rĕr′ ē/ –*adj.* For a limited time, not permanent: *The Coles lived in temporary housing until their new house was ready.*

Thurs·day /thûrz′ dē/ or /thûrz′ dā/ –*noun* The fifth day of the week.

tool /tōol/ –*noun* A device, especially one that can be held in the hand, used to carry out a task: *Ben needed a special tool to put the hinges on the door.*

tooth /tōoth/ –*noun,* plural **teeth.** Hard, bony structure in the mouth used for chewing food.

trea·ty /trē′ tē/ –*noun* An agreement between two countries, often about terms for peace or for trade.

tri·al /trī′ əl/ –*noun* **1.** An examination of the facts in a court of law to determine the truth. **2.** The act of testing something to judge its fitness or usefulness. **3.** Something challenging.

trust·wor·thy /trŭst′ wûr′ thē/ –*adj.* Able to be trusted, dependable, reliable: *Only lend your car to trustworthy people.*

Tues·day /tōoz′ dē/ or /tōoz′ dā/ or /tyōoz′ dē/ or /tyōoz′ dā/ –*noun* The third day of the week.

va·cant /vā′ kənt/ –*adj.* Empty or unoccupied: *We had to wait a month for the apartment to become vacant.*

va·ca·tion /vā kā′ shən/ –*noun* A time set aside for rest and relaxation: *I plan to sleep late every day during my vacation.*

ve·to /vē′ tō/ –*noun* The right of a president or other head of a government or organization to reject a law made by the branch of government that passes laws.

Wednes·day /wĕnz′ dē/ or /wĕnz′ dā/ –*noun* The fourth day of the week.

yield /yēld/ –*verb* **1.** To produce or give in return: *We hope the garden will yield lots of tomatoes this summer.* **2.** To give in or give up, surrender.

Personal Word List

Write any words that need more study. You can write words you see in this book, at work, or at home.

_____   _____   _____

_____   _____   _____

_____   _____   _____

_____   _____   _____

_____   _____   _____

_____   _____   _____

_____   _____   _____

_____   _____   _____

_____   _____   _____

_____   _____   _____

_____   _____   _____

_____   _____   _____

_____   _____   _____

_____   _____   _____

_____   _____   _____

_____   _____   _____

Alphabetical Word List

Word	Lesson	Word	Lesson	Word	Lesson
absorb	6	career	10	curious	24
accident	6	cause	8	damage	4
accuse	19	celebrate	15	dangerous	5
ache	5	challenge	21	debate	20
adjust	11	charge	3	decay	8
advancement	10	chill	6	deceive	3
advice	12	Christmas	15	decision	14
advocate	18	church	14	dedicate	15
agency	12	citizen	19	defense	20
annual	9	combine	23	define	21
apartment	2	committee	20	degree	24
application	1	community	14	democratic	17
appointment	8	company	9	dentist	8
approval	22	compare	3	department	14
arrange	23	complain	2	deposit	1
arrest	19	complete	16	determine	12
assemble	15	compliance	18	develop	10
athlete	7	comply	9	dictionary	21
attempt	11	computer	11	difficult	16
average	1	conclude	24	disagree	24
aware	6	condition	4	discuss	20
bank	1	Congress	20	dispute	19
behavior	24	consent	2	doctor	5
believe	22	consequence	8	document	17
benefit	9	constitution	17	duties	12
billboard	3	consult	8	earnest	12
booklet	16	continue	14	education	21
bottle	6	contract	9	electric	11
brainstorm	24	convention	17	emergency	16
break	4	convict	19	employ	12
breath	7	cough	7	enact	20
broken	6	coupon	3	energy	22
building	14	court	19	enforce	20
cabinet	20	credit	1	enormous	2

Word	Lesson	Word	Lesson	Word	Lesson
environment	7	interest	1	permit	2
equal	23	interview	16	poison	5
establish	10	iodine	6	practical	4
evidence	19	irritate	8	practice	21
exact	5	January	13	prepare	12
examination	19	justice	19	prescription	5
example	21	kitchen	2	probable	22
excellent	10	knowledge	3	produce	22
explain	10	label	23	promotion	10
extreme	5	legal	18	property	2
fail	21	liberty	17	public	14
fault	22	local	18	qualify	23
February	13	machinery	11	qualities	12
focus	23	manage	23	random	23
forbid	18	material	11	recognize	16
foreign	4	measure	24	recommend	8
Friday	13	Memorial Day	15	recycle	18
gallon	4	merchandise	3	refer	21
garage	4	merchant	12	reflect	24
gasoline	4	mileage	4	refund	3
government	14	miserable	8	regardless	16
growth	22	model	21	regulate	18
guide	22	modem	11	religious	17
habitat	18	Monday	13	representative	17
Halloween	15	money	3	requirement	14
healthy	7	natural	18	resident	2
heart	7	neglect	1	resource	23
historic	15	occasion	15	respond	1
holidays	15	occasional	5	retail	12
hospital	5	offer	2	retirement	9
hotel	16	official	15	reveal	22
imagine	24	opinion	22	review	10
improve	10	opportunity	7	revise	24
include	16	patriot	17	revolution	17
increase	1	percent	1	salary	9

Word	Lesson
Saturday	13
science	11
September	13
serious	23
settlement	17
signal	16
similar	7
sleepy	6
slogan	18
smoking	7
special	4
statement	21
strenuous	7
success	3
Sunday	13
superior	10
swallow	6
system	11
tablet	5
tax	9
teeth	8
temporary	14
Thursday	13
tool	11
treaty	20
trial	19
trustworthy	6
Tuesday	13
vacant	2
vacation	9
veto	20
Wednesday	13
yield	9

Answer Key

Pre-test

Pages 10–11: 1. B, **2.** D, **3.** C, **4.** A, **5.** B, **6.** D, **7.** A, **8.** B, **9.** A, **10.** D, **11.** A, **12.** C, **13.** D, **14.** C, **15.** D, **16.** A, **17.** C, **18.** B, **19.** A, **20.** D, **21.** C, **22.** B, **23.** C, **24.** D, **25.** A, **26.** D, **27.** C, **28.** C, **29.** B, **30.** A.

Unit 1, Lesson 1

Page 12: 1. respond, **2.** application, **3.** neglect, **4.** deposit, **5.** interest, **6.** bank, **7.** average, **8.** increase, **9.** percent, **10.** credit

Page 13: 1. v, a, average; **2.** c, e, s, increase; **3.** e, i, credit; **4.** e, l, e, neglect; **5.** d, p, s, deposit; **6.** e, o, n, respond; **7.** application, **8.** bank, **9.** increase, interest, **10.** percent, **11.** deposit, **12.** neglect, **13.** credit, **14.** percent, **15.** respond

Page 14: 1. dollars, **2.** windows, **3.** buses, **4.** forms, **5.** churches, **6.** pages, **7.** hours, **8.** dishes, **9.** foxes, **10.** averages, **11.** checks, **12.** loan, **13.** questions, **14.** tax, **15.** boxes

Page 15: percent, application, respond, average

Lesson 2

Page 16: 1. permit, **2.** kitchen, **3.** complain, **4.** apartment, **5.** offer, **6.** enormous, **7.** property, **8.** resident, **9.** vacant, **10.** consent

Page 17: 1–4. a/part/ment, re/si/dent, pro/per/ty, e/nor/mous **5.** complain, **6.** consent, **7.** permit, **8.** vacant, **9.** resident, **10.** offer, **11.** kitchen, **12.** enormous, **13.** property, **14.** vacant, **15.** resident, **16.** complain, **17.** enormous, **18.** complain, **19.** resident, **20.** apartment

Page 18: 1. (k)night, **2.** (w)rap, **3.** ca(l)f, **4.** bom(b), **5.** la(t)ch, **6.** shou(l)d, **7.** i(t)ch, **8.** fas(t)en, **9.** (k)nit, **10.** (w)rist, **11.** lim(b), **12.** ta(l)k, **13.** w, wrinkle; **14.** t, latch; **15.** b, limb; **16.** b, bomb; **17.** t, itch; **18.** l, talk

Page 19: resident, vacant, property, consent

Lesson 3

Page 20: 1. compare, **2.** refund, **3.** deceive, **4.** knowledge, **5.** charge, **6.** money, **7.** merchandise, **8.** billboard, **9.** success **10.** coupon

Page 21: 1. success, **2.** billboard, **3.** knowledge, **4.** merchandise, **5.** refund, **6.** money, **7.** deceive, **8.** charge, **9.** suc, success; **10.** ceive, deceive; **11.** cou, coupon; **12.** edge, knowledge; **13.** fund, refund; **14.** board, billboard; **15.** money, **16.** deceive, **17.** knowledge, **18.** success, **19.** billboard, **20.** charge

Page 22: 1. delivered, **2.** singing, **3.** allowed, **4.** coughed, **5.** jumping, **6.** brushed, **7.** called, **8.** seeking, **9.** sending, **10.** followed, **11.** telling, **12.** painting, **13.** pinching, **14.** spoiled, **15.** redeemed, **16.** returning, **17.** extended, **18.** trying, **19.** thrilled, **20.** thinking

Page 23: merchandise, coupons, tricking, knowledge

Lesson 4

Page 24: 1. gasoline, **2.** damage, **3.** mileage, **4.** garage, **5.** condition, **6.** special, **7.** practical, **8.** foreign, **9.** gallon, **10.** break

Page 25: 1. gasoline, **2.** mileage, **3.** foreign, **4.** gallon, **5.** special, **6.** break, **7.** damage, mileage, garage; **8.** break, **9.** condition, **10.** practical, **11.** break, **12.** garage, **13–15.** gas/o/line, prac/ti/cal, con/di/tion; **16.** e, i, foreign; **17.** o, i, gasoline; **18.** e, a, break; **19.** c, a, special; **20.** l, l, gallon

Page 26: 1. scent, **2.** wait, **3.** there, **4.** piece, **5.** lone, **6.** sent, **7.** their, **8.** weight, **9.** loan, **10.** peace

Page 27: 1. condition, special, damage, mileage

Unit 1 Review

Page 28: 1. A, **2.** D, **3.** C, **4.** C, **5.** A, **6.** C, **7.** C, **8.** B, **9.** A, **10.** D

Page 29: 11. B, **12.** A, **13.** B, **14.** D, **15.** A, **16.** B, **17.** B, **18.** A, **19.** D, **20.** B

PLEASE INSERT IN PLACE OF CURRENT PAGE

Unit 2, Lesson 5

Page 30: 1. hospital, 2. occasional, 3. extreme, 4. tablet, 5. dangerous, 6. ache, 7. exact, 8. poison, 9. prescription, 10. doctor

Page 31: 1. ache, 2. occasional, 3. exact, extreme; 4. prescription, 5. tablet, 6. dangerous, 7. hospital, 8. o, o, poison; 9. o, o, doctor; 10. x, a, exact; 11. l, e, tablet; 12. h, e, ache; 13. e, e, extreme; 14. i, a, hospital; 15. c, s, a, occasional; 16. (ocasional) occasional, 17. (pioson) poison, 18. (perscription) prescription, 19. (acke) ache, 20. (hospitel) hospital

Page 32: 1. brushing, 2. dated, 3. charged, 4. lifted, 5. writing, 6. driving, 7. playing, 8. moved, 9. shared, 10. losing, 11. opened, 12. using, 13. saved, 14. sharing, 15. giving, 16. stored, 17. placed, 18. tasted

Page 33: ache, doctor, occasional, taking

Lesson 6

Page 34: 1. chill, 2. swallow, 3. aware, 4. sleepy, 5. accident, 6. bottle, 7. absorb, 8. broken, 9. iodine, 10. trustworthy

Page 35: 1–4. ac/cident, swal/low, bot/tle, chil/l; 5. bottle, 6. broken, 7. sleepy, 8. accident, 9. chill, 10. trustworthy, 11. sleepy, 12. trustworthy, 13. broken, 14. chill, 15. absorb, 16. accident, 17. sleepy, 18. chill, 19. iodine, 20-22 ac/ci/dent, trust/worth/y, i/o/dine

Page 36: 1. u, n, unfair; 2. u, n, unhappy; 3. u, n, uncommon; 4. u, n, unbelievable; 5. u, n, unable; 6. u, n, uncover; 7. u, n, unlike; 8. u, n, unwanted; 9. u, n, unequal; 10. u, n, unkind; 11. u, n, unknown; 12. u, n, unusual; 13. rewrap, 14. recycle, 15. review, 16. recall, 17. rejoin, 18. reenter, 19. review, 20. unusual

Page 37: accident, sleepy, broken, aware

Lesson 7

Page 38: 1. heart, 2. breath, 3. similar, 4. healthy, 5. athlete, 6. opportunity, 7. environment, 8. cough, 9. strenuous, 10. smoking

Page 39: 1. e, t, healthy; 2. i, a, similar; 3. o, i, smoking; 4. l, e, athlete; 5. e, u, strenuous; 6. heart, 7. similar, 8. healthy, 9. breath, 10. environment, 11. opportunity, 12. strenuous, 13. healthy, 14. cough, 15. heart, healthy, 16. similar, 17. smoking, 18. strenuous

Page 40: 1. worries, 2. married, 3. copies, 4. studied, 5. pennies, 6. cried, 7. babies, 8. carried, 9. families, 10. hurried, 11. replies, 12. applies, 13. emptied, 14. puppies, 15. carried, 16. dried, 17. fried, 18. worries 19. families, 20. copies

Page 41: strenuous, heart, healthy, smoking

Lesson 8

Page 42: 1. teeth, 2. cause, 3. recommend, 4. dentist, 5. appointment, 6. consequence, 7. decay, 8. irritate, 9. consult, 10. miserable

Page 43: 1. consult, 2. miserable, 3. appointment, 4. teeth, 5. appointment, recommend, irritate, 6. dentist, 7. recommend, 8. miserable, 9. consequence, consult 10. decay, 11. recommend, 12. irritate, 13. consequence, 14. appointment, 15. (reccommend) recommend, 16. (teath) teeth, 17. (apointment) appointment, 18. (cauze) cause

Page 44: 1. mice, 2. children, 3. loaves, 4. deer, 5. men, 6. fish, 7. women, 8. feet, 9. geese, 10. sheep, 11. men, 12. loaves, 13. women, 14. mice, 15. children

Page 45: appointment, consult, miserable, recommend

Unit 2 Review

Page 46: 1. B, 2. C, 3. A, 4. A, 5. A, 6. C, 7. C, 8. A, 9. D, 10. D, 11. B, 12. C

Page 47: 13. B, 14. C, 15. A, 16. D, 17. C, 18. B, 19. D, 20. A, 21. B, 22. A, 23. B, 24. D

Unit 3, Lesson 9

Page 48: 1. contract, 2. retirement, 3. vacation, 4. comply, 5. yield, 6. tax, 7. benefit, 8. annual, 9. company, 10. salary

Page 49: 1. comply, contract; **2.** annual, **3.** yield, **4.** retirement, **5.** vacation, **6.** contract, **7.** salary, **8.** company, comply, **9–14.** sal/a/ry, ben/e/fit, com/pa/ny, re/tire/ment, an/nu/al, va/ca/tion, **15.** yield, **16.** tax, **17.** vacation, **18.** contract, **19.** annual, **20.** yield

Page 50: 1. library's, **2.** worker's, **3.** paycheck's, **4.** company's, **5.** Aaron's, **6.** saw's, **7.** meeting's, **8.** computer's, **9.** waitress's, **10.** manager's, **11.** The employee's health plan paid the doctor. **12.** The contract's meaning should be clear. **13.** Do not shut off the machine's power. **14.** Did you comply with your supervisor's request? **15.** Mary's goal is to get a better job.

Page 51: company, annual, vacation, comply

Lesson 10

Page 52: 1. review, **2.** develop, **3.** superior, **4.** excellent, **5.** improve, **6.** establish, **7.** explain, **8.** advancement, **9.** promotion, **10.** career

Page 53: 1. advancement, **2.** review, **3.** superior, **4.** promotion, **5.** improve, **6.** explain, **7.** explain, excellent; **8.** excellent, advancement; **9.** carear career, **10.** establesh establish, **11.** excellant excellent, **12.** d, c, e, advancement; **13.** e, o, develop; **14.** a, i, explain; **15.** o, e, improve, **16.** establish, **17.** excellent, **18.** explain

Page 54: 1. renew, **2.** exclaim, **3.** prolong, **4.** reappear, **5.** recount, **6.** disappear, **7.** express, **8.** proclaim, **9.** displease, **10.** discolor, **11.** propose, **12.** refill, **13.** excite, **14.** rebuild, **15.** dislike, **16.** rewind, **17.** reappear, **18.** dislike, **19.** rebuild, **20.** displeased

Page 55: Establish, excellent, Develop, advancement

Lesson 11

Page 56: 1. adjust, **2.** computer, **3.** system, **4.** science, **5.** modem, **6.** electric, **7.** attempt, **8.** machinery, **9.** tools, **10.** materials

Page 57: 1–5. ad/just, at/tempt, mo/dem, sci/ence, sys/tem; **6.** adjust, **7.** electric, **8.** tool, **9.** computer,

10. machinery, **11.** attempt, **12.** modem, **13–15.** adjust, attempt, computer; **16.** y, e, system; **17.** d, s, adjust; **18.** c, e, science; **19.** d, e, modem; **20.** t, a, material; **21.** t, p, attempt; **22.** o, e, computer; **23.** r, i, electric; **24.** c, e, machinery

Page 58: 2. the winners' prizes, **3.** the workers' health benefits, **4.** the teachers' lounge, **5.** the farmers' vegetable market, **6.** the wild horses' corral, **7.** the machine operators' rules, **8.** the registered nurses' uniforms, **9.** the customers' orders, **10.** the officers' meeting, **11.** the wolves' teeth, **12.** the guards' keys, **13.** Four of the clerks' reviews earned a superior rating. **14.** Lana studied the flight attendants' manual all day. **15.** Jade will explain the benefits of joining the employees' credit union.

Page 59: attempt, modem, materials, science

Lesson 12

Page 60: 1. earnest, **2.** merchants, **3.** agency, **4.** determine, **5.** advice, **6.** employ, **7.** duties, **8.** prepare, **9.** qualities, **10.** retail

Page 61: 1. retail, **2.** agency, **3.** prepare, **4.** determine, **5.** employ, **6.** qualities, **7.** advice, **8.** earnest, **9–15.** re/tail, mer/chants, em/ploy, du/ties, ad/vice, pre/pare, ear/nest, **16.** earnest, **17.** advice, **18.** employ, **19.** merchant, **20.** prepare

Page 62: 1. ., **2.** ?, **3.** ., **4.** !, **5.** ., **6.** ?, **7.** ., **8.** ?, **9.** !, **10.** ?, **11.** This is the most popular store in town. (or !) **12.** When is the best time to apply? **13.** Come quickly, the store manager is on the phone! (or .) **14.** I can start work next week.

Page 63: retail, merchant, duties, earnest; change? after buy; period; change period after you to question mark

Unit 3 Review

Page 64: 1. B, **2.** D, **3.** A, **4.** A, **5.** C, **6.** D, **7.** A, **8.** B, **9.** C, **10.** D, **11.** A, **12.** C

Page 65: 13. A, **14.** C, **15.** B, **16.** B, **17.** D, **18.** C, **19.** C, **20.** A, **21.** C, **22.** A, **23.** D, **24.** B

Unit 4, Lesson 13

Page 66: 1. Saturday, 2. Sunday, 3. Monday,
4. January, 5. Friday, 6. September, 7. Tuesday,
8. Wednesday, 9. February, 10. Thursday

Page 67: 1. Saturday, Sunday, 2. Tuesday, Thursday,
3. Wednesday, 4. Saturday, 5. January, February,
6. September, 7. Sunday, 8. Friday, 9. Wednesday,
10. d, s, Wednesday; 11. u, s, Tuesday; 12. r, i,
Friday; 13. o, n, Monday; 14. r, u, February; 15. S, u,
Saturday; 16. (Febuary) February, 17. (Munday)
Monday, 18. (Wensday) Wednesday

Page 68: 1. 354 N. Adams St., 2. Sat., Aug. 24, 1997,
3. 66 S. Lincoln Blvd., 4. Wed., Feb. 4, 1998, 5. 498
E. Madison Ave., 6. Thurs., Dec. 11, 1997, 7. 88 N.
22nd St., 8. Sun., Feb. 23, 1997, 9. West, Street,
10. Thursday, October, 11. North, Avenue,
12. Monday, November, 13. Saturday, August,
14. South, Road

Page 69: February, Wednesday, Thurs., Saturday

Lesson 14

Page 70: 1. community, 2. department, 3. government,
4. church, 5. continue, 6. building, 7. decision,
8. requirement, 9. temporary, 10. public

Page 71: 1. community, 2. department, 3. continue,
4. temporary, 5. government, 6. requirement,
7. church, 8. community, 9. temporary,
10. government, 11. continue, 12. decision,
13–15. re/quire/ment, gov/ern/ment, de/part/ment;
16. e, n, government; 17. i, c, public; 18. u, d,
building; 19. i, u, continue

Page 72: 1. payable, 2. excitement, 3. valuable,
4. placement, 5. manager, 6. action, 7. improvement,
8. acceptable, 9. conductor, 10. believable, 11. The
owner wanted $2500 for the car, but she would
take any reasonable offer. 12. The doctor said my
illness would not last long. 13. Pedro put on the
brakes, but an accident was not avoidable.
14. Before you can get a license, your car must pass
an inspection. 15. The batter did not agree with
the umpire's judgment.

Page 73: Community, government, temporary,
decision

Lesson 15

Page 74: 1. dedicate, 2. historic, 3. assemble,
4. celebrate, 5. holidays, 6. Memorial Day,
7. Christmas, 8. Halloween, 9. official, 10. occasion

Page 75: 1. occasion, 2. historic, 3. assemble,
4. Memorial Day, 5. Halloween, 6. Memorial Day,
7. Christmas, 8. dedicate, celebrate; 9–11. Memorial
Day, Christmas; Halloween; 12. f, c, official;
13. c, s, occasion; 14. s, l, assemble; 15. i, y, holiday;
16. C, a, Christmas; 17. e, a, celebrate; 18. celebrate;
19. dedicate; 20. officiate

Page 76: 1. I will meet Dr. Chin at the corner of
Lake Street and Columbus Avenue. 2. The
Christmas party was held in the Lawrence
Hillman Library. 3. Tuesday, Mr. Conners flew to
Ireland on Shamrock Airlines. 4. Sue will be in Los
Angeles for New Year's Eve. 5. The Bakersfield
Garden Club meets every Wednesday. 6. We will
have a costume party to celebrate Halloween.
7. The attack of Fort Williams was led by Captain
Logan. 8. Few passengers survived the sinking of
the ocean liner *Titanic*. 9. You must change to
another bus in Dallas, Texas. 10. The meeting with
Senator Davis was held on Tuesday.

Page 77: Memorial, Christmas, occasion, celebrate

Lesson 16

Page 78: 1. include, 2. signal, 3. hotel, 4. regardless,
5. emergency, 6. complete, 7. booklet, 8. difficult,
9. recognize, 10. interview

Page 79: 1. regardless, 2. signal, 3. booklet,
4. interview, 5. complete, 6. emergency,
7. recognize, 8. hotel, 9–13. in/clude, sig/nal, ho/tel,
book/let, com/plete; 14. interview, 15. include,
16. regardless, 17. (dificult) difficult, 18. (emergancy)

Page 80: 1. complete, emergency, hotel; 2. money,
signal, telephone; 3. examine, explain, factory;
4. church, comply, director; 5. annual, appeal, total;

6. dentist, percent, permit; **7.** apartment, avenue, garage; **8.** knee, knowledge, nobody

Page 81: emergency, regardless, complete, recognize

Unit 4 Review

Page 82: 1. B, **2.** D, **3.** C, **4.** A, **5.** A, **6.** C, **7.** D, **8.** B, **9.** C, **10.** D, **11.** C, **12.** A

Page 83: 13. C, **14.** B, **15.** A, **16.** B, **17.** D, **18.** C, **19.** B, **20.** A, **21.** D, **22.** B, **23.** C, **24.** C

Unit 5, Lesson 17

Page 84: 1. religious, **2.** democratic, **3.** constitution, **4.** representative, **5.** liberty, **6.** patriots, **7.** document, **8.** convention, **9.** revolution, **10.** settlement

Page 85: 1. religious, **2.** revolution, **3.** settlement, **4.** representative, **5.** convention, **6.** democratic, **7.** settlement, **8.** convention, constitution; **9.** representative, **10.** liberty, **11–16.** con/ven/tion, doc/u/ment, lib/er/ty, pa/tri/ot, re/lig/ious, set/tle/ment; **17.** i, u, constitution; **18.** o, u, revolution; **19.** i, o, religious; **20.** u, e, document

Page 86: 1. Did you study about the Boston Tea Party? **2.** One famous patriot was named Samuel Adams. **3.** Help is on the way! **4.** Where was the U.S. Constitution written? **5.** The convention was held in Philadelphia. **6.** Is that document important? **7.** We enjoy religious freedom in this country. **8.** I forgot we were having a history test today! **9.** She is our representative in Washington. **10.** This is a democratic nation. **11.** Where did you put that document? **12.** Never stop fighting for your ideas!

Page 87: democratic, representative, If you do, then vote for Steve Wells., patriot

Lesson 18

Page 88: 1. habitat, **2.** slogan, **3.** forbid, **4.** natural, **5.** advocate, **6.** regulate, **7.** compliance, **8.** recycle, **9.** legal, **10.** local

Page 89: 1. advocate, regulate, **2.** compliance,

3. habitat, **4.** legal, local, natural, **5.** recycle, **6.** legal, **7.** slogan, **8.** forbid, **9.** local, **10.** natural, **11.** ~~complience~~ compliance, **12.** ~~regutate~~ regulate, **13.** ~~forebid~~ forbid, **14.** ~~advacate~~ advocate;

Page 90: 1. preview, view before, **2.** illogical, not logical, **3.** compare, find what is like and unlike about two things, **4.** compress, press together, **5.** unusual, not usual **6.** review, view again, **7.** illegal, not legal, **8.** uncomfortable, not comfortable, **9.** prepare, get ready before, **10.** complete, to finish, **11.** unrealistic, not realistic, **12.** replacement, something put in place again

Page 91: Regulate, advocates, forbids, legal

Lesson 19

Page 92: 1. arrest, **2.** justice, **3.** examination, **4.** citizen, **5.** evidence, **6.** convict, **7.** dispute, **8.** trial, **9.** accuse, **10.** court

Page 93: 1. arrest, accuse, **2.** court, **3.** trial, **4.** dispute, **5.** examination, **6.** justice, **7.** citizen, **8.** convict, **9.** court, **10.** accuse, **11.** convict, **12.** dispute, **13.** evidence, **14–22.** cit/i/zen, ev/i/dence, jus/tice, dis/pute, ar/rest, tri/al, con/vict, ex/am/in/a/tion, ac/cuse

Page 94: 1. The judge ruled in favor of Mr. and Mrs. Kilpatrick. **2.** The court did not convict Dr. Wells. **3.** In court, Judge Davidson read the charges against Ms. Blair. **4.** Will Dr. Fishman's case go to trial? **5.** We asked Senator Thompson to give a speech. **6.** The judge gave Mayor Hudson the oath of office. **7.** It has been four days since Mr. Nashawati's arrest. **8.** The examination was given by Dr. Wu. **9.** Did Ms. Larson attend the trial? **10.** Our lawyer, Mrs. Clayton, will help us.

Page 95: Judge, trial, citizen, justice

Lesson 20

Page 96: 1. discuss, **2.** debate, **3.** cabinet, **4.** treaty, **5.** enact, **6.** veto, **7.** Congress, **8.** committee,

9. enforce, **10.** defense

Page 97: 1. cabinet, **2.** committee, **3.** Congress, **4.** Congress, discuss, **5.** enact, **6.** enforce, **7.** veto, **8.** treaty, **9.** cabinet, committee, **10.** i, e, cabinet, **11.** m, e, committee, **12.** a, y, treaty, **13.** e, a, debate, **14.** o, e, Congress, **15.** e, s, defense, **16.** (commitee) committee, **17.** (cabinit) cabinet, **18.** (treety) treaty, **19.** (enforse) enforce, **20.** (vetoe) veto

Page 98: 1. My Aunt Frieda lives in Duluth, Minnesota., **2.** I have never seen Lake Tahoe. **3.** Mrs. Marquez is from Peru, but her friend is from Mexico. **4.** The meeting was held in the Jones Arena. **5.** Will President Clinton attend the conference? **6.** I heard that Death Valley is the hottest spot in the United States. **7.** Her case went to the U.S. Supreme Court. **8.** Meet me at Maple Street near the Kennedy Library. **9.** We drive south as far as Crater Lake. **10.** Is Niagara Falls in New York?

Page 99: defense, committee, cabinet, Washington

Unit 5 Review

Page 100: 1. C, **2.** A, **3.** A, **4.** B, **5.** D, **6.** A, **7.** B, **8.** C, **9.** D, **10.** D, **11.** B, **12.** A

Page 101: 13. A, **14.** D, **15.** C, **16.** A, **17.** B, **18.** B, **19.** D, **20.** D, **21.** A, **22.** C, **23.** B, **24.** D

Unit 6, Lesson 21

Page 102: 1. example, **2.** statement, **3.** model, **4.** define, **5.** fail, **6.** practice, **7.** challenge, **8.** education, **9.** dictionary, **10.** refer

Page 103: 1. education, **2.** define, **3.** statement, **4.** dictionary, **5.** refer, **6.** fail, **7–12.** state/ment, re/fer, mod/el, de/fine, prac/tice, chal/lenge, **13.** l, e, example, **14.** e, l, model, **15.** l, e, challenge, **16.** e, i, define, **17.** education, **18.** example, **19.** refer, **20.** statement

Page 104: 1. break, **2.** coupon, **3.** cancel, **4.** eight, **5.** special, **6.** breath, **7.** cough, **8.** heart, **9.** fresh, **10.** yield, **11.** science, **12.** office, **13.** pioneer, **14.** journey, **15.** major

Page 105: refer, define, practice, example

Lesson 22

Page 106: 1. energy, **2.** believe, **3.** produce, **4.** growth, **5.** reveal, **6.** probable, **7.** approval, **8.** opinion, **9.** fault, **10.** guide

Page 107: 1. believe, **2.** energy, **3.** probable, **4.** opinion, **5.** approval, **6.** reveal, **7.** believe, **8.** growth, **9.** energy, **10.** guide, fault, **11.** approval, **12.** opinion, **13.** fault, **14.** guide, **15.** (fualt) fault, **16.** (gide) guide, **17.** (praduce) produce, **18** (beleive) believe

Page 108: 1. August 23, 1995, **2.** Tempe, Arizona, **3.** Detroit, Michigan, **4.** Miami, Florida, **5.** July 17, 1971, **6.** Albany, New York, **7.** October 10, 1969, **8.** Austin, Texas, **9.** February 14, 1994, **10.** Juneau, Alaska, **11.** On November 7, 1995, elections were held in every state. **12.** One candidate visited Miami, Florida. **13.** A rally is planned on October 10, 1998, in the Super Dome. **14.** The bus stopped in Stowe, Vermont, and Erie, Pennsylvania. **15.** Both candidates stopped in Nashua, New Hampshire, during the campaign.

Page 109: August 23, 1996, believe, approval, energy

Lesson 23

Page 110: 1. arrange, **2.** focus, **3.** combine, **4.** random, **5.** label, **6.** manage, **7.** qualify, **8.** resource, **9.** serious, **10.** equal

Page 111: 1. arrange, **2.** combine, **3.** resource, **4.** manage, **5.** equal, **6.** qualify, serious, **7.** equal, **8.** random, **9.** arrange, **10.** serious, **11.** e, l, label, **12.** o, u, s, serious, **13.** u, c, resource, **14.** c, u, focus, **15.** o, m, random, **16.** i, y, quality, **17.** arrange, **18.** qualify, **19.** manage, **20.** equal

Page 112: 1. Be sure to bring your notebook, pencil, and paper. **2.** Are you a doctor, a dentist, or a nurse? **3.** I love to jump in the pool, swim to the other side, and float on my back. **4.** The storm struck every city, town, and village in the state. **5.** I can work late on Monday, Tuesday, or Friday. **6.** The sport requires skating, blocking, and passing. **7.** Dr. Chu, Mr. Westover, and Ms. Gomez will arrange the meeting. **8.** The study will focus on Los Angeles, New York, and Chicago. **9.** I must work on Memorial Day, Halloween, and Christmas this year. **10.** We must decide on a time, a place, and a day for the rally. **11.** Rowena always carries a calendar, a notebook, and a pen. **12.** Identify your first, second, and third most important events.

Page 113: Arrange, Buy small, medium, and large envelopes., combine, Pick up milk, bread, and cheese for tonight., qualify

Lesson 24

Page 114: 1. brainstorm, **2.** measure, **3.** behavior, **4.** revise, **5.** degree, **6.** imagine, **7.** reflect, **8.** curious, **9.** disagree, **10.** conclude

Page 115: 1. disagree, **2.** conclude, **3.** curious, **4.** reflect, **5.** imagine, **6.** measure, **7–12.** brain/storm, meas/ure, con/clude, re/flect, re/vise, de/gree, **13.** brainstorm, **14.** reflect, revise, **15.** behavior, **16.** curious, **17.** measure, **18.** disagree, degree; **19.** dis, disagree; **20.** ous, curious; **21.** imag, imagine; **22.** hav, behavior

Page 116: 1. Sophia Tirpak, **2.** Mr. Samuel Reynolds, **3.** Personnel Manager, **4.** Performance Plus, **5.** colon (:), **6.** comma (,), **7.** between the city and the state, **8.** no

Page 117: curious, brainstorm, disagree, imagine

Unit 6 Review

Page 118: 1. B, **2.** D, **3.** A, **4.** B, **5.** A, **6.** C, **7.** D, **8.** B, **9.** A, **10.** B, **11.** A, **12.** D

Page 119: 13. C, **14.** A, **15.** C, **16.** A, **17.** D, **18.** C, **19.** A, **20.** B, **21.** A, **22.** D, **23.** C, **24.** A

Post-test

Pages 120–121: 1. C, **2.** C, **3.** C, **4.** B, **5.** A, **6.** B, **7.** B, **8.** D, **9.** B, **10.** A, **11.** C, **12.** A, **13.** A, **14.** D, **15.** B, **16.** C, **17.** A, **18.** B, **19.** D, **20.** C, **21.** A, **22.** B, **23.** A, **24.** B, **25.** C, **26.** D, **27.** A, **28.** B, **29.** B, **30.** D

Scoring Chart

Use this chart to find your score. Line up the number of items with the numbers correct.

For example, if 14 out of 15 items are correct, the score is 93.3 percent.

Number Correct

Number of Items

	5	6	7	8	9	10	11	12	13	14	15	16	17	18	19	20	21	22	23	24	25	26	27	28	29	30
5	100																									
6	83.3	100																								
7	71.4	85.7	100																							
8	62.5	75	87.5	100																						
9	55.5	66.7	77.7	88.9	100																					
10	50	60	70	80	90	100																				
11	45.4	54.5	63.6	72.7	81.8	90.9	100																			
12	41.7	50	58.3	66.7	75	83.3	91.7	100																		
13	38.5	46.1	53.8	61.5	69.2	76.9	84.6	92.3	100																	
14	35.7	42.8	50	57.1	64.3	71.4	78.5	85.7	92.8	100																
15	33.3	40	46.6	53.3	60	66.7	73.3	80	86.7	93.3	100															
16	31.2	37.5	43.7	50	56.2	62.5	68.7	75	81.2	87.5	93.7	100														
17	29.4	35.3	41.2	47	52.9	58.8	64.7	70.6	76.5	82.3	88.2	94.1	100													
18	27.8	33.3	38.9	44.4	50	55.5	61.1	66.7	72.2	77.8	83.3	88.9	94.4	100												
19	26.3	31.6	36.8	42.1	47.4	52.6	57.9	63.1	68.4	73.7	78.9	84.2	89.4	94.7	100											
20	25	30	35	40	45	50	55	60	65	70	75	80	85	90	95	100										
21	23.8	28.6	33.3	38.1	42.8	47.6	52.3	57.1	61.9	66.7	71.4	76.1	80.9	85.7	90.5	95.2	100									
22	22.7	27.3	31.8	36.4	40.9	45.4	50	54.5	59.1	63.6	68.1	72.7	77.2	81.8	86.4	90.9	95.4	100								
23	21.7	26.1	30.4	34.8	39.1	43.5	47.8	52.1	56.5	60.8	65.2	69.5	73.9	78.3	82.6	86.9	91.3	95.6	100							
24	20.8	25	29.2	33.3	37.5	41.7	45.8	50	54.2	58.3	62.5	66.7	70.8	75	79.1	83.3	87.5	91.6	95.8	100						
25	20	24	28	32	36	40	44	48	52	56	60	64	68	72	76	80	84	88	92	96	100					
26	19.2	23.1	26.9	30.8	34.6	38.5	42.3	46.2	50	53.8	57.7	61.5	65.4	69.2	73.1	76.9	80.8	84.6	88.5	92.3	96.2	100				
27	18.5	22.2	25.9	29.6	33.3	37	40.7	44.4	48.1	51.9	55.6	59.2	63	66.7	70.4	74.1	77.8	81.5	85.2	88.9	92.6	96.3	100			
28	17.9	21.4	25	28.6	32.1	35.7	39.3	42.9	46.4	50	53.6	57.1	60.7	64.3	67.9	71.4	75	78.6	82.1	85.7	89.3	92.9	96.4	100		
29	17.2	20.7	24.1	27.6	31	34.5	37.9	41.4	44.8	48.3	51.7	55.2	58.6	62.1	65.5	69	72.4	75.9	79.3	82.8	86.2	89.7	93.1	96.6	100	
30	16.7	20	23.3	26.7	30	33.3	36.7	40	43.3	46.7	50	53.3	56.7	60	63.3	66.7	70	73.3	76.7	80	83.3	86.7	90	93.3	96.7	100